CONTENTS

MOTORCYCLE TOURING

"Why Don't I Come With You?"

By

Chris Hardy

IT'S FOUR IN THE MORNING...

The rough route, we did tend to wander off it.

Maybe if you are lucky enough in life you will experience a couple of moments of sheer joy. The first time your child smiles up at you as you hold it in your arms, discovering radium and winning the Nobel peace prize, or even successfully managing to invade the stage at the Redcar bowl after drinking ten pints of Newcastle Exhibition to join "The Sensational Alex Harvey Band" in singing two lines from "Delilah".

I myself have managed two of those moments, admittedly one of them didn't end well (never trust a group of smiling bouncers if they are leading you to the fire exit) but you get the gist. It's those moments when all is right with the world and you bask in the warm glow of life.

Fortunately if you happen to own a motorbike you won't have to suffer years of lost sleep and empty pockets, die of radiation poisoning, or spend your life with a miss shaped nose to reach those peaks. These moments will instead come with alarming regularity, looking at your bike parked on top of an alpine pass with snow-capped mountains in the background, opening the tent after a nights wild camping and waiting for the sun to dry it's seat as you drink your coffee, or even just opening the garage to nip down to the local Aldi on it, and all of this before you even get your arse on the seat and start her up.

Unfortunately staring out from the bedroom window at 4.00am in the morning and watching the rain hammering down onto its waterproof cover knowing you have a three hour ride ahead of you to the ferry does not earn a place in "The sheer joy of owning a motorbike" handbook.

As I made my way back to bed silently cursing both my bladder and the weather I heard my girlfriend's voice in the darkness.

"Is it raining?" she muttered with that false note of concern people have who won't be getting on a wet bike and trawling down the motorway waiting for the cold water to enter their waterproofs and slide around their genitals to grip them like a small squid in its clammy cold embrace. In fact she doesn't even have proper genitals, well she does but not like a blokes that hang about outside because hers are all tucked away (if you don't know this please be very careful in your drinking habits when visiting a certain street in Thailand). Women really don't know how lucky they are.

"Of course it is, I'm getting on the bike, it always rains when I get on the bike, and I have to get on the bike in the rain because I have to get to Venice airport, and the reason I have to get to Venice airport is because you will be flying into that airport to begin your holiday with me, but of course it won't be raining in Venice will it? Oh no, the sun will be out and you will wander down the steps carrying nothing with you but your helmet and an air of nonchalance after a couple of hours in the air while I have trawled half way across bloody Europe dragging all your clothes and......" I didn't actually say this of course.

"Yes bunny, it's raining" I whispered.

"I'm sure it will stop before you go" she said as she patted my back, rolled over, and went back to sleep.

She snores by the way.

Okay I have to make something clear here as this book is about two up touring, our lass (my girlfriend for those of you who are not from the north) is great. It was actually my suggestion that she flew into Venice as this would gave me a few days on the bike to myself while on the way to pick her up. We had done this on a few occasions and it worked quite well, I enjoyed the time to myself and she loved arriving at the airport with an air of nonchalance carrying only her crash helmet in her hands. Anyway, let's go back in time so I can explain how we got to this point shall we.

THE WALL

If you have by any chance read one of my other books on this subject you will know the process I go through when deciding where and how to get to where I wish to go so I won't blather on about the process here. To cut it short I am fortunate enough to have my own space with a very large map of Europe on the wall where I sit in my swivel chair and ponder on a route. This time however the process was taking a longer time than usual due to the fact we had a cat sitter for as long as we wanted (within reason).

Now not having enough time is bad, but having too much time can actually bring problems as well. A year is great for zooming off round the world, two weeks is fine for zipping around Europe, five weeks however poses something of a quandary. Anywhere was within our reach but because of our method of touring it fell into the "not quite long enough" and the "a little too long bracket". Let me explain, we are not the "Yeah we did 400 miles yesterday" couple. We are more like the "Stop stop...can we climb up there and eat lunch" couple (which turns into two hours of laying in the grass lost in our thoughts and pondering on how amazing this world is). We can spend an hour drinking a quick cup of coffee and another hour watching Eagles soaring overhead, and when we stay somewhere we like to leave knowing the place and the people who live there.

The other problem was we had been quite a few places already and I hate back tracking on a route, so that was why I was sat staring at the map with a blank expression on my face. Eventually I settled on a visit to Corsica, over to Sardinia, and maybe the ferry down to Sicily. I spent nearly a week finding the best airport for her, best routes for the bike, and best (and cheapest) places to stay. It was perfect, and as we were going in June it wouldn't be too crowded and the meandering route to and from the holiday spots were a bikers dream.

I then decided against it for some reason that I can't remember now.

This formed a pattern for the next couple of weeks, I would find a route, explain it to her, she would say "Lovely" and I would then find some reason why it wasn't quite right. This exasperates our lass, I once asked her why she never seemed very excited when I told her of all the amazing places we would be visiting and she said "Chris, everywhere we have ever been has been wonderful but until we actually set off and get there I never know if it's where you said we were going". She does have a point I suppose.

Things were further complicated by the fact that I had decided to splurge a bit of money on this trip. Normally it's a case of packing the tent, buying cheese and ham for lunch as we wander the back roads, being ever mindful of how much a coffee costs, and moaning about the price of a kebab. I have to reiterate at this point about how great our lass is, even when she is being eaten alive by flying things (they love her as much as I do) or sitting in a tent listening to the rain hammering down she never moans or sulks. I would rather have her on the back of the bike than anyone else on the planet due to this amazing forbearance she shows when things don't go quite right. She also comes with the added bonus of not being bloody huge so she only takes up a small amount of space in the tent, her packing takes up less room, and she's not putting undue stress on the bikes suspension, yeah she's not bad our lass. Anyway this time I was going to treat her to a roof over her head for every night of the trip, admittedly the places we would be staying wouldn't have air conditioning or room service as I wasn't made of bloody money. On the point of money, if your lass works (or in my case she has a nice pension) make sure she goes half's on everything. I have never understood this "The man pays for everything" business, ye gods what the hell is that about? I would never and have never demeaned a woman by paying for her drink, meal, or holiday as I have far too much respect for them to do that.

Where was I? Oh yes, I had decided to forego the

pleasure of being a tight wad just as an experiment to see how it felt and to see if I was actually capable of spending money like other people apparently do. This in part was one of the problems when it came to picking a route for this trip. "I'm not paying that!" and "You must be bloody joking, £40 a night! Who pays that sort of money just to sleep in a bloody bed?" were often heard booming from the room according to my dear Theresa. Eventually I found what I thought was a good route around Europe that would combine all the things we liked and presented it to Theresa, my equal in status partner in life. (Okay enough of that, I'm sorry but if any feminists or PC lovers are reading this you are just going to have to suck it up because the effort involved in not calling her "our lass" is making me miserable so "our lass" she shall remain ... forever).

I would set off a week before her flight and make my way across France and Italy to pick her up at Marco Polo airport (flight costing £22, which she paid for out of her own money by the way) and from there we would take the following route.

Italy, Slovenia, Austria, Czech Republic, Germany, France, maybe Belgium if I could be bothered, France, and then a little tour of England's bottom.

"Lovely" she said.

"No darling, that is the route for definite, honestly, this time it really is" I said.

"That's lovely then" she said. I gave up ... and then altered the route again without telling her.

Chris Hardy

The thing is, and this is in my defence here, when I go with our lass I suddenly feel something I have tried to avoid most of my life but with only limited amounts of success, responsibility.

When I go off on my own I really don't give a toss where I stay, where I end up, or what happens, being on the road brings its own joy for me. Now when I plan a route taking Theresa it's all different, I want every day to have a moment, a sight, or an experience she will be astounded by. Rubbish I know, everyday can't be astounding but when it isn't, I feel as if I have buggered up, even when logic and Theresa tell me I am being an idiot. That I suppose is the thing you have to bear in mind when taking someone with you, well I do, you might not be as idiotic as me.

… OF MICE AND MEN

So again, if you have read one of my other books you will know all about the stuff I carry, how I plan the route, why I sometimes don't wear underpants or socks, and why too many sweeteners in your coffee can be a very bad thing. Therefore I have no intention of slapping it in at this point and boring you all over again, instead I will leave it until the end of the book so you can ignore it if you wish. I will however mention the bike we use to roam the roads. It's a 2007/8 V-Strom 650 with 60,000 miles on the clock, slightly beaten about and grey in colour. If you are thinking about getting a bike to wander off on you can't do much better than one of these. Cheap to run, reliable, comfortable, easy to work on, and it can stand being dropped without falling to pieces. It isn't full of electronic gizmos being an earlier model and for me that's a bonus (do you really need something to help you with hill starts for god's sake?) The good thing about not taking all the camping stuff was there was no need for the huge panniers that came with the bike. We got all we needed for five weeks away into the top box and a couple of cheap soft Oxford panniers I bought from EBay for £10 and we still had room to spare.

We shall now return to that fateful morning of departure.

I had decided to catch the afternoon ferry to Cherbourg and stay the night there due to it arriving at 19.30. I wasn't in any rush and wanted to while away the evening wandering the port as I had always just zipped through it on my other trips. This course of action was imagined taking place on a balmy evening with the sun dipping gently down to the sound of young people's laughter as I drank coffee at a charming cafe and posed in my £2.49 sunglasses. The reality turned out to be little different.

"It might stop" she said as I tugged at the crotch of my waterproofs and opened the front door. "Oh there's no doubt about that" I said casting a sarcastic glance backwards as the door opened to reveal a river of water flowing down the gutter. We kissed and I bumped the cup of tea I had made her, spilling some onto my boots. "Oh you got tea on your boots" she said with a look of concern. I cast my second sarcastic look of the day and patted her head. "I will see you in a week cupcake, bye bye". I noticed she closed the door rather quickly, not wishing to get her slippers damp no doubt.

I sat myself onto the bike, tugged at my crotch again, and pushed the starter settling myself in for a long wet ride. Three hundred yards later I pulled into the petrol station, weeks of faffing about and planning and I had forgotten to fill the bloody bike up. It's strange how something so unimportant as filling the tank can make you so miserable. Off came the gloves, off came the helmet, out came the keys, faff about getting the wallet out, faff about putting the helmet on, faff about putting now wet gloves back on, faff about with my bloody crotch again (and it's never as comfy as it was before you got off the bloody bike) jab the keys back in, reset the mileage, press the starter, engage gear, let the clutch out, and then realise you still have the bloody side stand down.

The only thing I can say in favour for trawling along in the rain whilst on a motorbike is that it feels so bloody good when you get to the end of your journey. Arriving at the ferry terminal I was relieved to see there was only two other bikes there (I'm not big on talking to other bikers I'm afraid) and I managed to get to the toilet and back without being accosted and having to indulge in mind numbing banter about knee downs, torque, low down grunt, or how much someone's boots cost.

While standing by the bike reflecting on life and attempting to roll a fag with wet hands something dawned on me, I loved my life. Now this wasn't a new revelation but I was always amazed at the odd moments this thought arrived in my head, at this moment I was wet, cold, and my underpants were soggy. I looked at the huge posh camper vans and shiny new cars in the other lanes with their warm dry occupants and couldn't quite grasp why I would never swap places with them. It makes no sense does it? You must feel the same way surely. What the hell makes us do it? You are either too hot or too cold, you get wet, your arse gets numb if you sit on it for too long, and everyone is trying to kill you as soon as you put it into bloody gear. And don't get me started on how much the bloody things cost. It makes no sense when we could be in a nice warm car surrounded by a safe environment and cup holders. I lost myself so deeply in this musing that I failed to hear the tramp of motorbike boots until it was too late.

"What do you think of those Michelin road 5s then" he said.

Twenty minutes later I had learned all I could ever wish to know about where he had been, how long it took him to get there, how many bikes he had owned, how long he had been riding, and yes, even where I should go even though I had told him I had already been. Even when he asked me a question it was only a trick so he could tell me more about himself. Thankfully I was saved by the call to board.

Look I am a bit anti-social okay and I make no apologies for this as I understand where it comes from. If someone is funny or interesting I could listen to them all day but talking about bikes after about three minutes just numbs the brain, unless of course it contains a sentence like "For fecks sake don't ever pull the clutch in and turn the hazard lights on at the same time because that model of bike has a tendency to explode when you do that". Then there are the older blokes who get out of their cars and slowly edge towards you like a sly seagull after your chips, now a word of advice if you are like me, never NEVER even glance at them because that is the only opening they need and the next words you hear will cast a shadow of dullness onto your once bright life. "I used to have a BSA, it was many years ago mind and the wife wouldn't put up with me having one now" he will say with a chuckle. I know all this makes me sound like some total knob but … ye gods I have been staring at the screen for five minutes now trying to think of what to say in my defence on this subject and can't come up with anything. Bugger.

The boarding was as the boarding always seems to be, I parked the bike in the appointed place, re-moved the rubber bands and plastic bag from my satnav (it's just a £30 car Garmin from EBay but with a rubber band and a freezer bag it suddenly be-comes as good as a £350 waterproof bike one) and set off to find a quiet place to eat the ham and cheese sandwich our lass had made for me that very morn-ing.

The Channel tunnel is great to get to France but there is something about taking the ferry that makes you feel as if you are actually going somewhere special. I love watching people and the ferry is a perfect place to indulge this pastime. Now don't get me wrong, I am not a leering "Look at the chest on that" type of person, I just like watching people because they are funny.

The "New age dad" who talks about what he is doing with his kids in a voice loud enough to inform the whole area about how engaged he is with them. The old couple sat sharing the crossword. The group of men that always seems to have one that's the butt of all the jokes. Then there's the family of five not eating the massively overpriced ferry food because they are too busy on their phones.

I had a little wander on deck because the rain had stopped, then departed the deck because the rain started again. I should really invent some amazing experience here to keep you entertained but sometimes travel includes periods of introspection and quiet solitude that holds no terrors for me. I think that's part of the attraction of motorcycle travel, if you do it alone for long enough you start to discover things about yourself, begin to accept your true self, see your faults, and I suppose (and I know how creepy this might sound) learn to love yourself despite them. Well I think I should change the subject now before we get all touchy feely and start lighting joss sticks.

As we are stuck on this boat for a few hours I might as well mention my bike in a little more detail. As I have said it's a 2007/8 Suzuki V-Strom 650.

It really is a great bike, seriously. If someone said he would swap me for a brand new BMW I would take him up on the offer and then go straight out and sell the bloody thing to buy another V-Strom (thus pocketing a nice lump of cash to spend on petrol). Even at the most basic level my old bike beats a brand new one hands down. Here's an example. While boarding, two aforementioned BMWs pulled up beside me, who (going by all the kit they were wearing/carrying) must have been off to tour Africa for six months. Now I can simply hoist my leg off the bike, hang my helmet on the mirror, and walk away. Not so the BMW riders. They have to inspect their bikes while cleaning off as much surface water as possible with a rag specifically designed for this purpose then wait for the crew to strap their bikes down and carefully inspect the man's work for any scratches and tightness of straps.

Obviously riding a BMW you have to have all the gear to go with it so there now follows the concern for helmets, sat navs, packing of their BMW branded jacket, and removal of their BMW "moving from one place to another while off the bike" jacket to wear on the boat. I kid you not as I have seen all this with my own eyes on several occasions. So a big downside for me to own a brand new (unscratched) hugely expensive bike would be all the faffing about that goes with them. I mean a scratch on one of them could ruin the poor bugger's trip, on mine it would be just another mark to remind me of where I had been.

The other good thing about my bike is it feels like it's mine, probably because it is mine and not just something that has to hold resale value for the next one in two years' time or handed back under the PCP deal. I can work on it myself, drill holes in it for 12v sockets (I was in danger of getting carried away with this and Theresa had to hide my drill in the end) and even re-spray the bits that get knocked. The joy of owning a bright new shiny thing is limited, owning something that can truly become a part of you makes the joy last forever ... well until the bloody thing falls apart that is.

Well not much about the bike in that chunk of prose, but what can I say about it really that I haven't already said. It's got a great tank range, it's great on fuel, comfy seat, it's great two up once you get an extension piece from Cymark to kick the top box back so a pillion can fit on the bloody seat when the top box is fitted. (www.cymarcbike-parts.co.uk). Does anyone actually try these things before they start selling them? I mean come on, my girlfriend is a size 10 and found it impossible to get comfy before I moved the box back and you couldn't even get the bloody seat off with the top box on. Seriously, get an extension bracket if you buy an older V-Strom. It handles well (the bike that is, not the extension bracket) goes fast enough to keep up with everyone else, and it even has enough space under the seat to carry a small child (give it a go if you have one, they will love it).

Ah yes, one fault I did find was with the headlights. Due to the starter dragging all the power it can from the bike it kicks the lights off when you press it. This can bugger up the copper strip connector in the starter switch resulting in the lights not coming back on. Easy fix though, just strip the switch, clean the connector, and slap some grease on it (I use Vaseline). Just be careful not to lose the damn spring that fly's out like a cruise missile. If you do just put a spring in from a ball point pen (fortunately I had a ball point pen when this happened to me in a tiny village miles from anywhere in Portugal). Enough of all this, let's get on with the trip.

HANG ON ... IS
THAT LIVER?

It was pissing down when we pulled into Cherbourg and as I followed the other bikes into France I wished I had taken the time to give my visor a rub. Coming up to the very first roundabout I watched as the first bike joined it, then the second, then the third, and just as he set off I saw him look the wrong way. The sound of horns, the biker stops too sharply on his front brake, and slowly tips over in front of the approaching car. I stop, help him up (he didn't want to talk and couldn't see the funny side of it) and I bid him farewell. No harm done apart from bruised pride I suppose.

I spent the short wet ride to my Première Classe hotel (€26) trying to remember how many times I had dropped my bike and looked like a numpty and came to the grand total of six. One of the worst (but not THE most embarrassing) was when I first started riding. I had a new job and the boss pulled up next to me just outside the factory gates. To chat to him I got off the bike (a GS125) and simply held the clutch in while it was still in gear. Feck knows why I did that but you can maybe guess the rest. We chatted for longer than I expected until eventually he opened the gates and drove in. I went to get on the bike but twisted the throttle accidentally and my hand slipped on the clutch. The feckin bike shot off and upwards like a scalded cat, I lost my grip and it set off towards my new boss's car. Fortunately it collided with the gate post and I managed to grab it and pretend absolutely nothing had happened just before my boss closed his car door and waved at me. What a twat.

My dreams of wandering aimlessly around the port drinking coffee in my new shorts and Aldi sunglasses had come to nothing. Instead I sat in my room looking out onto the car park and the industrial estate beyond wishing there was a Buffalo Grill within striking distance. The rain was now hammering down and next door the group of French window fitters were getting drunker and louder by the minute. Great start to the trip I thought to myself. Fortunately I wouldn't starve as I always carry a few "Expedition Adventure meals". Now don't they sound exciting? In fact they really are quite good but don't get the beef hotpot, its bloody awful.

Ah, the romance of life on the road.

I showered, set up my camping stove, put some music on from my phone, and settled down to spend the evening sending inane messages to our lass and reading free books from amazon on my second hand Kindle (£6 from EBay). Tonight it would be tales of excitement and adventure from H. Rider Haggard.

Where I stayed; Première Classe Cherbourg. 382 Rue Des Pommiers, 50110 Cherbourg en Cotentin, France.

Verdict; if you have never stayed in one of these don't expect room service or a photo opportunity for the bike. They are clean (generally) inexpensive (most of the time) and normally close to a "Buffalo Grill" (this one wasn't which very nearly broke my heart). It is a bed for the night, nothing more and for me when I am alone that's fine, anything better is a bonus. One point, sometimes the French Government rents blocks of rooms for immigrants, do not be concerned by this. I once spent a wonderful evening in a Première Classe car park surrounded by people from every African country you can imagine enjoying the fruits of an impromptu barbeque they had set up. Just chill my mate.

I awoke feeling refreshed and keen to start the day, until I opened the curtains and saw it was still hurling down with rain. This posed a problem because I had planned my route as a meandering wander along scenic roads while stopping at roadside cafes to enjoy the ambiance of quaint French villages. This lost its charm for me as I watched the rain bounce off the car park and I realised I had all day to do about 200 miles to my next stop. This isn't a bad distance if the weather is nice but I could see myself arriving at my destination with nothing to do and only a boring trip to look back on behind me. I suppose if I hadn't booked my next night's stay I could have travelled further but the Pension I was heading for was the cheapest I could find in quite a large area (€28 compared to a ridiculous €50) so for a man who was careful with his money I was a bit stuck. Anyway I dragged myself into my waterproofs, packed the bike, sighed, and set off to join the day.

The best and most exciting thing that happened on the journey was finding a Carrefour with a petrol station and bus stop attached, this meant I only had to stop once for fuel and had a pleasant place to prepare and eat my lunch. It wasn't the best bus stop I had stayed in but it was dry and there was plenty of room for my cooker and even a hanger (an old rusty screw) to hang my wet gear up on. I was joined at one stage by a sweet old couple and we shared quite a few laughs together although I have no idea what about as I couldn't understand a word of what they said (and I suspect they never understood me either). We parted as friends when the bus arrived and they waved from the window when they took their seat. Once again I adjusted my crotch, hoisted myself onto the wet seat, and set off with an expression fixed in stone.

Where I stayed; Carrefour.
Verdict; Don't be daft.

Montigny-le-Gannelon was my destination and it was lovely. Little streets, a large chateau, old church, beautiful old farm houses, there was even a large lake on the outskirts, everything you could wish for to enjoy a stop over. Apart from a shop, or a café, or indeed a restaurant, these omissions from the village did not worry me unduly as my Pension also had a restaurant and I looked forward to spending some of my money on an evening of fine dining.

I had arrived too early to check in (by about four hours) so decided to spend the time exploring the chateau. I was quite used to the rain by now and the soggy socks and wet underpants barely registered in my consciousness as I plodded through the puddles to arrive outside the imposing gates. They were shut. "It is of no never mind" I thought to myself, "I shall explore the fine interior of the 13th century church instead". It was shut. Ah well I thought, I shall wander the outskirts of the village and maybe bid "Bonjour" to some friendly locals. It was shut. If you have ever passed through France you must know this phenomenon, nothing shuts like a French bloody village. Where do all the people go? What do they know that I don't?

I looked down the steep hill that led into the non-beating heart of the village and realised I was in a bit of a fix. My darling girlfriend will confirm I have no problem with walking about for a bit, I don't even mind walking down a hill if there is something at the end of it, it's the walking back up that I find ruins the whole experience. I decided there was nothing in the village worth the effort and settled down on the wet grass under a tree to watch some rather forlorn ducks waddling around the small pond by the church. This trip was not exactly going as I had imagined but my Pension looked nice and a good warm meal would sort me out as it always did.

I could just see the Pension from my vantage point and decided to see if I could gain entrance a little early. A note was pinned to the door and with my limited knowledge of French I managed to make out the following message. "We are shut (no surprise there then) and will not open until 18.00.

25

Please do not bang on the door as there is no one here". I trudged back up the slight incline, resumed my position under the tree and returned to watching the ducks. Eventually 18.00 came and bang on time the owner arrived to open up. We exchanged details and I asked what time the restaurant opened as I was by now bloody starving. "On Thursday at 19.30" he replied smiling proudly. Today was a Wednesday.

I dragged my bags upstairs, took the cooker out again, and tried to decide between a crushed pack of noodles with a sachet of tomato sauce I had nicked from McDonalds many moons ago, a sardine sandwich, or another "Adventure meal". I had to admit the "Adventure" aspect of the meal was starting to wear a little thin as these things should be eaten on a mountain or in a deep wild forest, not a bedroom with flowered wallpaper. The owner had informed me he could prepare a breakfast for me if I wished and I was all for it, until that is he told me the price. The next morning I sat in my bedroom and tucked into my dry bread and sardine sandwich with forced relish. €7 indeed, he must have thought I was a fool with pockets lined with gold and nothing between my ears if he imagined I would pay that.

Where I stayed: Le Relais de Montigny. 19 rue Grande, 28220 Montigny-le-Gannelon.

Verdict; On a better day it would have been fine, owner was nice, bed comfy, village quaint, and it should have been a good stop for the night. It wasn't mainly be-

cause of my mental attitude and the bloody weather.

Next morning it was raining of course but I knew it would be, it was turning into one of those trips. My destination for the day was Guegnon where I had found a nice place with a restaurant (that was open) and breakfast included for €28 Waterproofs on, plastic bag over the Satnav, helmet on, wet gloves on, press the starter and the phone goes "Bleep". I was so tempted to just ignore it but I knew it would bug me so ... gloves off, waterproofs unzipped, jacket unzipped, glasses on, phone dragged out of freezer bag, and ... she had sent me a picture of the bloody cat. The caption read "She's so cute". I didn't send a reply.

I got lost in Orleans, drenched in Nevers, and slightly depressed in Decize. Then amazingly the rain slowed to a drizzle and I realised I had been singing to myself for at least on hour, I had crossed into my personal nirvana at last.

Nirvana: a transcendent state in which there is neither suffering, desire, nor sense of self, and the subject is released from the effects of karma and the cycle of death and rebirth.

Looking back I think the problem arose because I had expected to be miserable when I set off and so, like a self-fulfilling prophecy, I was. I can't really understand why I set off in this mood on this particular trip, the human brain is a funny thing. Anyway, it was over and from here on in I began to just roll with the journey.

Guegnon was dry when I arrived and I found street parking just up the road from the hotel and what's more it was a proper hotel with a sign and a bar, and even a lift. I felt I had turned a corner. I unpacked and wandered off for a walk before stuffing my face. I didn't get far because I found myself in the middle of a huge row that was going on between a bunch of commuters in their cars and a scaffolding company which was blocking the main road through the town with their lorry. My new friend and I (a rather rotund old French man with a stick and a beret) rested against the bridge wall and watched the chaos surrounding us with glee.

The lorry was trying to reverse into a covered courtyard with very limited room and refused to give ground to the honking cars trying to get past. Fortunately his mates thought they could help more by berating the drivers instead of actually watching him as he backed in. My new friend and I conducted our conversation using only our hands and shoulders. He would shout encouragement in French to whichever side seemed to be losing ground or thinking of giving up, spurring them on to new levels of righteous anger. I was just shouting "Allez Allez" at the top of my voice simply because, well it just seemed apt in the situation, and as I have mentioned my knowledge of the French language is very limited.

Eventually the lorry entered the courtyard and to a crescendo of horns the commuters drove on their way. As we parted my new friend raised both his hands and gave a classic Gallic shrug, I did the same.

The restaurant was now open and I took my place picking the "Plat de jour" and not bothering too much about the translation of what was on offer. I ended up with a liver salad to start. Now call me a sheltered soul but I had never had a salad covered in liver before, I mean who came up with that one? It was actually bloody lovely and the liver was nothing like the stuff my mother used to drop onto my plate and force me to eat. I can't even remember the main course or the dessert I was in such a state of shock.

After dinner I wandered into the bar and joined the locals pondering on why eating and drinking alone has never bothered me. I could come to no real conclusion as I had nothing to measure it by, I had never really felt uncomfortable traveling or eating by myself, in fact at a lot of levels I relished it. Maybe it was my deprived childhood, or meeting a group of insanely great drinking mates when I was younger and who I have never found a match for (I went back to my roots quite a few years ago to find virtually all of them are now dead from drink, drugs, or suicide). Do I get lonely? Yeah but it's that sweet loneliness. Just the thought of setting off on a tour with a group of other riders is an anathema to me. And yet as I watch the group of locals at the bar laughing and sharing a long common history I feel a huge sense of loss for my long dead friends. I order another beer and take it outside to roll a cigarette and watch the night descend over the town, melancholy seeps into me and I smile as a burst of laughter erupts from the bar.

"Here's to you my old mates" I whisper as I flick my cigarette stub into the bucket, raise my glass, and swallow the last dregs.

Where I stayed; Hotel Restaurant Saint-Benoit. 7 Rue Du Port, 71130 Gueugnon.

Verdict; It's a hike to the room but there is a lift so that's not so bad. On street parking but if that really worries you maybe you should ride a less expensive bike. The food is great and not a bad price, the waitress is a feast for the eyes, and the locals are friendly. Not much to do in the town but there again I couldn't be bothered to go exploring (if you want a breakdown of every historic building and point of interest buy a bloody "Rough guide" you tight sod). Yeah all in all a decent stop, and as with all my places to lay your head it won't cost you much.

FRENCH KEBABS

It was a good spread at breakfast, now I like a fry up but I have to admit a good continental breakfast is slowly becoming my favourite start to the day. One of the reasons is it's really hard to stuff your pockets with bacon, eggs, and sausages whereas it's easy to fill them with a couple of cartons of yogurt and a few ham and cheese rolls. The coffee was rubbish though as it always is in France but because of my need for copious amounts of the stuff through the day I filled up with it anyway.

My next scheduled stop was Vizille where I had found a rather dubious looking hotel right in the town centre for €23. Amazingly it hadn't rained now for over two hours but I suspected this was simply because I hadn't gone near the bike in that time. Breakfast finished and pockets stuffed with my lunch I carefully made my way with bags in hand towards it, checking the sky all the time like a wary Meerkat. Nothing, not a sign of precipitation could I see, in fact there was even some signs of blue up there. I skipped back across the road, paid the bill and went upstairs to collect the rest of my gear. It was pissing down by the time I got back downstairs. Bollox.

The rain stayed with me on my way to Lyon and kept me company as I got insanely lost in the back streets of that fair city. One wrong turn is all it took and I was completely stuffed and what's more I desperately wanted a wee. Getting lost in a city is bad, getting lost in a city in the hammering rain is worse, getting lost in a city in the hammering rain while holding your bladder really is the bloody pits. My destination was now of no importance, I tried relaxing, but a tiny bit of wee came out, my mind was now in complete shut down and I missed a café, I cursed myself, called myself names, rode like a complete lunatic and wanted to kill every other person on the road. Finally another café appeared in front of me and I swung right across the road to dump the bike in front of it. It was feckin shut. I couldn't get back on the bike as hope had filled my bladder even further so I set off hop waddling down the road and there right in front of me was my salvation. Through the door opening my jacket as my eyes raked the room for the toilet, there to the right, into the toilet waterproofs pulled down, two more strides, poppers pulled, zip down, todger out and oh my God how wonderful does that feel. I swore to myself right then and there I would stop drinking so much coffee.

Ten minutes later while I was sitting at the counter drinking my coffee I realised I had left the keys, helmet, gloves, and satnav on the bike.

With a now empty bladder I found the road I wanted straight away, amazing isn't it how easy something is when you are comfortable. It stopped raining just as the Alps came into view which was something of a relief. Every time I had ever crossed them it had been pouring down, no matter what time of the year or which route I took it was always in the bloody rain. As I sat looking at them in the distance while eating my slightly soggy ham and cheese rolls at the Aire De Repos near La Frette I thought that this time I just might get to see the buggers. I stuffed my waterproofs into the front crash bar bags (£2.99 on EBay from China. Look for the push bike ones as they fit just as well and don't come with the stupid price tag of anything with "motorbike" attached to it) and set off for my last stop before Italy.

Could I find that hotel, could I buggery, and when I did find it I had no idea how to get to it. Eventually I parked the bike and walked the roads to try and work out the labyrinth of dead ends and one way streets. Finding a route I loaded it into the steel trap that is my memory and got back on the bike, immediately forgetting if it was left at the third turn or right. In the end I just rode up onto the pavement through the pedestrian only area and nobody seemed to be very bothered. (When I left the hotel the route was obvious even to the Satnav, it wasn't complicated at all, it was simply my total ineptitude).

The manager at the hotel made me put the bike in their garage which was such an unaccustomed luxury for it that I could virtually feel its bewilderment. Now the town of Vizille has a few things going for it, it's on the Route Napoleon, it has a huge chateau, and … well I suppose if I am honest that's about it. One thing it shares with every other place I have ever visited in France is its inability to understand how to make a decent kebab. Now I like a kebab (something the lovely Theresa understands and suffers in silence) and I have eaten them in many countries. Poland - lovely and a good price, Latvia - strange but just as good, Portugal - great, Czech republic - very nice and a reasonable price, Nova Scotia - huge but not very tasty, Germany - lovely, Austria - a little too hygienic, Slovenia - fantastic, Belgium - weird but there again the whole country is, Spain - consistently great (the very best one I have ever had in my life was in Seville) Italy - no problem with them, Croatia - a decent kebab, Montenegro - they can be forgiven for not grasping the idea properly but still very tasty, France - consistently bloody awful. How do they not understand what a kebab should be like?

Anyway if you stay in Vizille at the hotel Sandra don't exit the hotel turn left then right and get a kebab from the shop on the corner, in fact don't buy a kebab anywhere in France. I am of course willing to change my opinion so if you know of a good one send me the address for God's sake.

That's about the sum total of my discourse on Vizille apart from the fact I met three British bikers who were also staying at the hotel. They were going somewhere and had come from another place, which was nice.

Where I stayed; Hotel Sandra. 46 Rue des Docteurs Bonnardon, 38220 Vizille.

Verdict; A lot better than I thought it was going to be, okay the room was a bit tired but I had a balcony for God's sake and the bike was in a nice dry garage. The owner was great and the bed was comfy and the shower was hot.

Next stop would be Susa in Italy, now this was only about 100 miles away but it was over the mountains and into Italy so I planned to take my time and explore as much as I could, and bugger me, as soon as I crossed the Italian border the sun came out, birds began to sing, and the coffee suddenly got better. The day was a sheer joy, great roads, waterfalls, snow-capped mountains and amazing views. I pulled into Susa feeling refreshed and alive for the first time on the trip.

Chris Hardy

My bed for the night was in a large convent that was home to a bunch of lovely old nuns. The doors were locked at 22.30 and after that there was no way in but this was a small price to pay for the pleasure of staying in such a clean welcoming place, and

I was normally sound asleep by that time anyway. I must admit I have reservations about nuns since I spent some time in a Catholic care home as a child but you can't tar everyone with the same brush and all the ones I met here were lovely, unlike some of the buggers from my youth.

Susa is a great place to explore and I regretted my decision to only stay for one night (£20 including breakfast), I even found a great kebab shop that amazingly enough sold "Super Bock" beer (next time you are in Portugal give it a go, you won't regret it). I wandered the town for a while and then returned to spend some time relaxing in the convent gardens. A small group of youths were practicing Brazilian drumming for a forthcoming festival when I arrived and the sound was amazing. A group of nuns had gathered to listen and I watched as they began to gently sway to the rhythm, smiling in their sandals and innocent pleasure. As I left one of the older nuns asked if it was my bike parked in the car park and we chatted for a while about where I had been and what my favourite places in Italy were. It turned out she was from one of the towns I knew quite well (Treviso) and we talked about how it had changed over the years.

Breakfast was great and they had even printed out a small prayer for my journey and placed it on my table. I am not a great believer in all that gibberish but every little helps when you are on a bike so I placed it in my wallet. The sun was now beating down and I finally removed my second layer before slipping on my jacket. It's strange how everything changes with the sun, with warmth, with blue, blue, skies. Your body discovers a new fluidity, a smile forms inside and refuses to leave, and when you kick that bike into gear for the first time as you set off you get that little thrill running right through you. I started to sing "Hollywood nights" by Bob Seger, and knew it was going to be a good day.

Me, on a good day.

Where I stayed; Casa per ferie Centro Beato Rosaz. Via Madonna delle Grazie 4, 10059 Susa.

Verdict; this was a gem of a place, the bed was comfy, the showers could strip your skin if you wanted them too, the room was immaculate, and the nuns were great.

The place is huge with gardens you can walk in and it's bang in the middle of the town, I really should have stayed longer but I tend to want to keep moving. The breakfast really was good and ... well it was just one of those slightly odd places you find that tends to fit perfectly with something inside of you. Okay there is a curfew (around 22.00 if I remember rightly) and the interior is a bit stark so if you want to come back rolling drunk at 2 am or need a luxurious ambiance go somewhere else, but for the money it was great. Oh and there's lots of pictures of Jesus and Mary looking down on you so try and keep the swearing to a minimum please.

One other thing, they had no idea who Father Ted was.

Theres a cafe on the left that sells "Ichnusa" beer, lovely.

LIKE VENICE
USED TO BE

My next stop was a small town called Pizzighettone about 150 miles away but I spent so much time wandering up and down mountains it took all day to reach it. Once you hit the flats heading west or east in northern Italy you have two choices, spend a fortune on toll roads or spend hours wandering the small slow "SP" roads. I never (or virtually never) spend any time on toll roads in any country (apart from Austria as it's so cheap for a bike it's daft not to buy the sticker) for a few of reasons. I am a tight wad, I like twisty roads and scenery, and I have nothing but time. A lot of the time avoiding toll roads on this route can be slow and frustrating but on this day the gods smiled down on me. Traffic melted away and every road I picked rose up to greet me. Some days are just perfect for no great reason, they just are. The sun feels warmer, the breeze gentler, and the people you meet friendlier than on any other day, the bike sang along with me as I tipped it into the corners and rode towards the plains of Italy.

Now this might sound pathetic but there really is something really cool when you are roaming the twists and turns of a mountain road and you manage to share a very low victory sign with a passing biker, even sticking your leg out as you pass has an intrinsic coolness. Transfer this sign of acknowledgement to our country and simply because we ride on the other side of the road all we have is "The Nod". As I ride alone I dread a convoy of bikers coming the other way as I end up looking like a demented bloody chicken whereas on the continent a long slow low "V" sign is … well it's just so bloody cool. Yeah having written all that down it does sound quite pathetic but hell, it just feels so good doing it.

Coming up to an old bridge I saw the speed signs advising me to drop down to 20km and as I was in such a chilled out mood and the road was empty I took no notice of it whatsoever. The bloody thing was cobbled, it was a bridge covered in cobbles that had been laid by a blind drunken Albanian who couldn't understand Italian and was suffering from the worst hangover in the history of hangovers. The bike was going down as I was going up, it was going left as I was going right and we only shook hands briefly after about three hundred yards. Only luck (and maybe that prayer I had slipped into my pocket) saved me from a rather stupid slide down the road that would have ended the trip there and then. I gathered my wits, shook my head, and reminded myself not to ride like a twat again for the foreseeable future.

Very nearly a bridge too far.

Pizzighettone is a small typical old Italian town split by a river surrounded by now incomplete defensive walls. It also has a great place to stay (€29) and an equally great restaurant next door. I arrived in 32c heat so dumped the bike and stripped down to my shorts to wander the streets until I could check in. I don't think it's on any tourist map, there are no great monuments or places of interest there, but if you like friendly cafes, shady walks by the river, and the sound of children's laughter it might be the place for you.

Much to my regret (the consequences of which will play on my mind for a very long time) and due to my dawdling I missed one of the main yearly cultural events to take place in this village. I have placed a picture of the events winner below but looking at it again I seem to find it rather disturbing for some reason. At first glance all seems well but as it draws you in you seem to enter a world that is slightly askew.

And I missed it ...sigh.

My evening meal was consumed in the restaurant two doors down from the B&B and consisted of the set menu, I have no idea what I had but I do remember it was a good evening, the food was brilliant, and I didn't cry when I paid the bill. The man who owns it used to be a copper and from where I was sitting I caught sight of the calendar behind the bar, each month depicted a scene from some aspect of police work and so as I waited I flicked through it. There was the murder scene, the hit and run scene, the crowd control scene, and amazingly the forensic lab scene, I stopped at that point. It made a change from kittens and puppies I suppose but I did hope I didn't get a liver starter again. He also had a riot baton above the bar fixed onto the wall, I left a tip.

I now had a decision to make, I had a spare night to while away before I picked Theresa up and needed to find something within my self-imposed price range that held some interest for me now the weather had broken and I could wander around properly. I retired to the local café, ordered a beer, and searched the area via Google. I had visited a lot of places in the area and wanted somewhere I hadn't been before, as it was getting hotter I either wanted to be high up or by the water, eventually I found what turned out to be a gem of a place in Chioggia.

Where I stayed; Residenza La Torre. Via Sortita 5, 26026 Pizzighettone.

Verdict; Look if you don't stay here if you are in the area there is something wrong with you. This place was not only cheap enough to satisfy my demanding stand-

ards, it was also bloody luxurious. The room, the village, the river, the restaurant next door, the owner, the break-fast, everything was right up there with the best places I have stayed at. The only bad thing was not having our lass with me because she would have loved it. The bike has to be parked in the village car park but that just makes for a nice photo (look forget about your bike, no-body is going to nick the bugger). Oh just don't be a smart arse with the owner of the restaurant, he's a lovely bloke but doesn't suffer fools gladly.

One end of my street in Chioggia.

Chioggia is just south of Venice and looked like what I wanted so I found a decent looking hotel and booked it for the night. It would mean a very short ride to Marco Polo airport the next day but I figured I could while away the time easy enough.

The ride there was just as good as the previous day and I took advantage of it to the full. I lunched on warm cheese, warm soft bread, and spicy salami on the steps of an old deserted farm house surrounded by olive trees. I skipped stones across Lake Garda, drank coffee and ate cake in Ferrara, and sat watching the river Po flow out into the Adriatic. By the time I got to Chioggia I was possibly one of the most contented men in Italy.

My hotel was at one end of a small street butting onto a canal with typical Venetian bridges crossing over to typical Venetian houses and at the other end of the street the fishing boats moored to drop their catch. I have been to Venice three times in the past, twice out of season (when there was an out of season) which were great and once in season which was so bad we only spent a couple of hours there before jumping back on the train. This place was like a smaller version out of season Venice only in season, if that makes sense. The locals still held sway here and workers still filled the cafés, this was my kind of place.

The owner of the hotel wouldn't hear of me leaving the bike in the street and made me place it in the rear yard, I can honestly say in all my travels I have never had any problem leaving the bike anywhere but I suppose it's always nice when someone takes the trouble to offer a safe place for it. While I was tucking it into the corner a couple of Polish bikers arrived (they told me their names but I am buggered if I can remember them or even spell them if I could) and we had a chat. It turned out they were from Wroclaw and by an amazing coincidence I had spent a week there a couple of years back. I asked if the brass gnomes were still okay and if the all you can eat buffet was still open, they laughed when I told them I always went 30 minutes before it closed because they took 50% off the price. "No one is that much of a skinflint" they said, they had only known me for ten minutes and we had the language barrier to deal with but I think they were convinced by the time we parted.

I (finally) spent the evening in my £2.49 Aldi sun glasses wandering the canals, listening to buskers playing classical music, sitting on church steps eating ice cream, and watching the fishing boats set out for the nights fishing. It was such a magical evening I even phoned Theresa and never thought once about how much it was costing me … well okay I did think about it once but I still did it.

This is what I think touring is all about, getting to know where you are and where you have been, not just ticking off places for a bucket list "Instagram" page or to show what a wonderful life you lead to your mates on "Facebook". I admit I fell for all that crap at one stage until I realised I was missing the moment, I was experiencing a magnificent sight and yet not being truly there. Maybe if I explain when the realisation came to me it will make more sense.

A few years ago I was on the ferry to Spain and

as sometimes happens I was unable to sleep so I wandered up onto the deck (it was about 5am) and leaned over the railings. Suddenly a whole pod of porpoises appeared at the stern tearing along hunting tuna fish. It was a staggering sight, porpoise flinging themselves out of the water, tuna cutting through the surf like sodding Exocet missiles and the boat rocking along only feet away from them. I grabbed my camera and put it onto video staring intently at the screen to make sure I got the best shot possible to put up on Facebook. For a moment I turned to see if anyone else was privy to this amazing sight and to my surprise at the far end of the railings … a young girl was just staring into the water, no camera, no phone, nothing but her mind was recording the view. My hand slowly dropped and I got it, I regained my sanity, it was like a weight falling from my shoulders.

It really is so easy to get sucked into all that crap and forget that the only time that really exists is this very moment, this second that your eyes are scanning over this word … and now it's gone. Sure I take pictures to share with my 32 friends on Facebook, but I very rarely post pictures of the truly magical moments, because they are mine, and mine alone.

Now here's another thing, for years I believed those porpoise were hunting the tuna, it turns out I was wrong, it turns out Tuna actually swim with them for safety. Now you could say it was a simple mistake to make and leave it at that but when I learned the truth I again realised how easy it is to place your trust in a falsehood, a lie. I know this has bugger all to do with anything, it just really gets to me when it happens, makes me feel a complete fool, anyway sorry for jumping the thread, I shall now carry on with the tale ...

Where I stayed; Domus Clugiae. Calle Luccarini 825, 30015 Chioggia.

Verdict; €20 including breakfast and the breakfast was the best I or we had on the tour, it took up two rooms, one for sweet stuff and one for savoury. The owners were really good, the location was brilliant and the atmosphere was friendly. The area as I have mentioned was just perfect with local cafes full of local friendly people. I just loved the place.

The other end of my street.

The best food, best company, and (for a while) best table cleaner in Chioggia.

WAITING FOR
A PLANE

The next morning I packed the bike and rode it all of three hundred yards to the local café by the fishing boats where I spent two hours watching the old men playing dominoes and conversing only as old Italian men can converse. Somehow I found myself clearing tables for the old woman behind the bar much to the amusement of the establishment's patrons. Eventually and with a heavy heart I said my good-byes and dragged myself away to head for Venice and to pick up my lovely pillion.

I had booked a room weeks ago for this night and had stayed there before so I knew there was no problem booking in early but it was such a nice day it still took me all day to cover the short distance to the hotel. Theresa wasn't due to land until around 18.00 so I had plenty of time and decided to find a nice place to check the bike over and do a bit of chain maintenance. This took longer than normal because every time a car, bike, or truck went past they would honk their horns to see if I had a problem. The constant waving and smiling eventually got on my nerves and I decided to finish the job in the hotel car park. The rooms at the hotel are above a pizzeria which serves the best pizza in the whole area. It's called "Colors" and is situated on the Via Orlanda with a bus stop right outside if you fancy a trip into Venice itself.

Unpacked and showered I had nothing to do apart from sit on the veranda overlooking the main road and watch the world go by (which is one of my favourite exercises). The airport is only five minutes up the road from the hotel and I fully intended to wait until Theresa sent me a text stating she had landed before I set off. Ten minutes later I was at the airport a full 30 minutes before her plane was even due to land, I must be getting soft because I couldn't wait to give her a hug. I had picked her up from this airport before and it's one of the better ones for the purpose because there's a petrol station just at the bottom of the car parks where you can park the bike and lay on the grass (don't try doing it in a car though as the attendant will chase you off).

As I waited I got into a conversation with a man who had just flown in from Nigeria. He was one of the biggest blokes I had ever seen and when he laughed his whole body shook like a huge (and very muscular) blancmange. He also had the rather unfortunate (for me) habit of slapping me on the back whenever I happened to say something even slightly amusing. Eventually a rather tired looking

Honda Civic arrived to pick him up which was a little complicated as it was already full to capacity with four other equally huge Nigerians and their luggage. I can still hear their booming laughter as they rammed him and his battered suitcase in and across the back seat. I watched as the poor ill used car dragged itself to the roundabout, and then dragged it's self all the way back. The rear window came down and the giants head appeared, "Goodbye my friend" he shouted roaring with laughter. "Goodbye my friend and vaya con Dios" I shouted back. This caused him to roar with laughter again for some reason, which can't have been good for the cars suspension. Silence descended on the petrol station after the car vanished to its unknown destination, no trace of the laughter or companionship two strangers had shared for a short time remained, apart that is, from the fact the memory of our encounter will stay with both of us.

In a movie I would see Theresa in the distance, she would drop hers bags and we would stare at each other for a moment before running in slow motion into each other's arms, I would then sweep her up and spin her round as we kissed. Maybe even music would erupt from the Tannoy system and the people around us would spring into dance.

Instead my phone went off "Where are you, I can't remember where the petrol station is" she said. "I'm here" I said rather unhelpfully. She didn't drop her bags as she never had any and there is no way she would drop her crash helmet, we didn't run in slow motion towards each other although I did manage a slight jog for a moment to get across the road, and there is no way I was going to sweep her off her feet, not with my back. We did have a little snog though and she romantically whispered into my ear "Have you been eating garlic?"

So, that's the story up until I picked our lass up and the real trip began. We ate too much pizza that night, slept soundly, and awoke ready to spend the next five weeks having a nice wander about on the bike.

Where we stayed; Colors. Via Orlanda 66, 30173 Campalto, Italy.

Verdict; I love this place, I think it's the staff more that the room or how good the showers are because they are after all, just a room and a shower for the night. It's the staff though that make this place shine out and I must admit I got a warm glow when the manageress remembered us and showed Theresa and I her baby that was only a bump the last time we were there. The pizzeria is a joy to eat in and not only gives your palate a taste of Italy but your senses also. The place is a family concern and everyone who eats there seems to become a member of that extended family by default. The only downside is the damn pizzeria is shut on a Tuesday evening.

A BIT OF ITALY,
A BIG CHUNK OF
SLOVENIA

O r destination for the day was Hotedršica in Slovenia, a small village west of Ljubljana where I had found what promised to be a nice stay for the night. It wasn't too far (about 130 miles) so we had plenty of time to stop off and chill. The road out of Italy from Venice isn't very interesting and we had done it a couple of times before but our lass got a few thrills as the marsh land we passed was full of herons, egrets, and a load of other flapping things. I knew she was happy because she kept informing me of this fact by wrapping her arms around me, slapping my sides, and shouting "Heron" into my helmet. We don't have an intercom system, just hand signals and at lower speeds shouting. I don't think either of us feels the need to talk to each other all the time as we are both content with our own thoughts.

I had decided as usual to avoid all the main roads on this trip and this led us through hot deserted small villages and quiet lanes. The roads didn't really get interesting until we crossed the border to join the 207 and then it slowly started to rise and twist. Theresa started taking pictures, twisting to one side and then the other while holding her camera in both hands and only settling into her seat when I warned her of upcoming hairpins, which now thankfully started to appear with regular frequency.

Just a note here concerning the pictures in this book, if they were printed in colour the bloody thing would have cost you over a tenner so I thought to hell with that, this isn't a first edition of something by Shakespeare for gods sake, it's just something to keep you amused until the pubs open or you have to do the washing up. Anyway, I hope they give you some idea of how amazing the places we visited were.

"I used to drive one of those Theresa"

The village of Hotedrsica was only small but it packed a lot in, old barns full of wood, beautiful churches, traditional Slovenian hay racks, a small stream, and all surrounded by beautiful country-side disappearing into the mountains. There was also a huge amount of renovation going on in the village, the main road was being upgraded and quite a few houses were being painted and re-roofed. This isn't a tourist place, maybe in the winter it would fill up with the skiers but in the summer it is just a typical Slovenian working village. As we entered the village the road vanished and was replaced by hard core and rubble with a red stop sign blocking our way which was a shame as I could see our hotel just up the road. We waited patiently as you do and then not as patiently as you do. As we were wait-ing a beaten up old Volvo approached from behind and paused next to us, the driver enquiring without the use of any vowels what so ever as too why we were blocking the road. I pointed to the stop sign at which point he laughed and shouted pointing at us "English" then pointed at the ground "Slovinia" and proceeded to just ignore the stop sign. He did have a point, not a car had passed apart from an old tractor and we were in the back of beyond. I suppose that may be a difference between our way of life and other countries, they still have the ability to just use common sense. I tapped it into gear and drove to the hotel shaking my head at the stop sign and my rigid adherence to the rules of the road.

The hotel was a ski lodge looking type of thing that had been in the owner's family for a few generations and as much of the food served at the table was either local or came from his family farm. Now I am not great at appreciating food (as witnessed by my obsession with kebabs) but I can tell when it's good and everything we had here was simply bloody amazing. Take the ham and eggs I had for lunch as an example, now in England if you order ham and eggs you can picture what you are going to end up with can't you? Okay now take that plate of ham and eggs and throw it out of the nearest window because I now know what we get served doesn't come close to what ham and bloody eggs should either look or taste like. It was bloody lovely, I relished every mouthful, I didn't want to swallow the last mouthful in fact and I didn't until our lass started getting annoyed with me for not swallowing it. Theresa had some beetroot salad with pumpkin oil poured over it, now I personally wouldn't go anywhere near such food but she assured me it was amazing as well. I am not going to harp on about every meal we had on this trip because it would bore me to tears but (always a "but" in life) the venison and dumplings I had for tea and our lass's Idrija Zlikrofi was even more amazing. Now in England if you wanted food this good it would cost a fortune and be served by some bugger in a white shirt and a stupid looking beard. Here the service and value was so good I even left a tip.

That evening we sat on the veranda listening to the rolling thunder in the distant mountains and watched the farmers driving their old beaten up tractors home from the fields, a perfect end to a perfect day.

Next morning I woke early and checked the bike over replacing some oil it had burnt on the trip out. I carry half a litre in those front crash bar bags ever since I had to buy some from a garage in Italy a few years back, €22 for ½ a litre, I kid you not. I still keep the container in the shed with the price tag on to remind me just how cruel life can be.

Breakfast (I know I said I wouldn't go on about food but bear with me) was one of the best I had ever eaten, thick local cured meats, scrambled eggs the colour of corn, homemade bread, and glorious coffee by the pot full. I stuffed myself until I couldn't move, our lass was a little more sensible.

Where we stayed; Gostilna Turk. Hotedršica 28, 1372 Hotedršica, Slovenia.

Verdict; what an incredible level of quality for the money, it was staggering. The owner was one of the nicest blokes I have come across on my travels and we parted I hope good friends. The food is superb, service fantastic, and the room was beautiful. I don't say all this because I liked the owner, I say it because it's just true.

Better than plastic wrapped hay bails.

INTO THE VALLEY ...

The road into the Logar valley.

W e had been to Slovenia before but had stuck to the Triglav area due to time constraints so this time we decided to wander about a little more. We were heading for a place I had found in a small village called Luce near the Logar valley. Now this was only about 60 miles away and some might think that is a pathetic distance for a day's travel, but once you have been to Slovenia you will understand why it can take so long to travel such a short distance, and to give you a taste here is the note Theresa made in her journal of the day.

"Had an amazing breakfast (it was huge) and set off for Luce. A beautiful ride in rich countryside, green fields with huge wooden barns and traditional Slovenian hay racks, allotments full of vegetables just plonked in the middle of a field. We are surrounded by tree covered mountains with snow-capped ones in the distance. Small beautifully tendered colourful villages, Austrian type houses all maintained and painted in subtle type colours with low sloping roofs and verandas covered in geraniums and petunias. Each village has at least one church with ornate black towers usually on the higher ground set apart from the village. Switchback swooping ride along amazing roads, Very hot by 12.00 but okay if we kept moving, its 15.00 and we haven't eaten since breakfast, still full!"

The ride there, the road, the people we met, and the views were stunning. Eagles flew above us and the sun beat down on our backs, what more could you want from life.

Having stolen the description of the ride to Luce from Theresa I think I will steal more from now on. I knew Luce was a wonderful place but if you asked me why I doubt if I could remember all the reasons. Having read our lass's diary it all came flooding back so here's what she had to say about Luce.

Our Wendy house.

Luce. Found our chalet, it's just like a little Wendy house, small but with everything we need for the next five days. Mountains surround us and a fast flowing crystal clear turquoise river runs along one side of the village. We are next to the village wood yard and at the bottom of the garden are two fat happy pigs. The owner of the chalet said we can pick our salad from the garden, made ham and cheese rolls with the lettuce! Took a walk along the river, it has a huge wooden waterfall. At the top end of the village there is what looks like an open air museum made from small traditional wooden huts containing all the crafts that were prevalent in this area. Amazing village.

Every day we spent there I remember crawling into bed thinking "Well that was amazing, tomorrow can't get any better than this", but it did.

Even when the weather turned the next day and the rain lashed, the lightning flashed, and the thunder roared above us, we had a great day because we just slapped on the waterproofs and went walking in the hills, sheltering in an old barn when the rain threatened to swamp us. We rode to Krajinski National Park when the sun came back and visited the beautiful Logar valley.

Rinka waterfall in the Logar valley.

Now if you ever visit this place I defy you not to stop as soon as you pass the gate and take a picture of your bike with the road stretching out in front of you. This has to be one of the most beautiful places I have ever been, huge grey snow topped mountains, wooded valleys, and the Rinka waterfall where the water forms a rainbow as it falls in a narrow band 90m into a crystal clear pool. The road there and back was undergoing repair and it was great how they dealt with it. The road was ripped up and all the cars simply drove around the machinery on the hard core base. No traffic lights, no closure signs, just once again, common sense.

"I used to drive one of those Theresa!"

Every morning we would walk down to see the pigs, walk up through the village past all the chickens, have a coffee, and buy our supplies for the day. On one of our walks we met Anna, the girl who had created the small open air museum at the end of the village, and she kindly (and free of charge) walked us round the site explaining about all the various crafts that every village had back in the day. She invited us into the old farm house they had transported there log by log and rebuilt as a meeting place where she fed us homemade cheese and bread. Our lass had some Zganci (made from buckwheat, corn, wheat or barley and then pressed (I kept well clear of it) and loved it (there's nowt as queer as folk if you ask me). Anna was, and hopefully still is, lovely. She had gone off to work in Ljubljana but couldn't cope with the lifestyle so returned to create the museum with little or no help from the authorities and to work on her parent's farm.

The next day was Slovenia's statehood day so the flags were flying and all the villages we passed on the way to Velika Planina were setting long tables out for the celebrations. It took us twenty minutes on the bike to reach Velika but over two hours of climbing to get to the plain itself. Now as I have mentioned before I am not a fan of walking up hill but I have to say this time it was worth it. Any description I placed in here wouldn't do it justice and would ramble on forever so just "Google" it to get an idea of what you are missing. If you don't want to do the hill climbing rubbish there is a cable car that staggers up but it cost's money, hence the reason I spent over two hours dragging my ass up there.

Even I have to admit it was worth the walk.

Luce was full of flags and bunting by the time we got back and a stage had been erected by the waterfall for the evening's festivities. There was plenty of beer but no drunks and everyone sang old patriot folk songs about something or other with words that had a lot of consonants in them but no vowels whatsoever, it was a good way to end or stay in the village and we walked back to our Wendy house by torch light.

Where we stayed; Apartments Sobe Jurček. Luče 51, 3334 Luče, Slovenia.

Verdict; Again a really good place to stay as long as you get on with your partner because the apartment we had (it was the cheapest) really was like a Wendy house. It had everything you could need including a decent kitchen and the space was enough as long as you didn't want to hold a party or escape a moody loved one. The area was brilliant, and the owner was great.

Luce, even in the rain it's magical.

... AND ON TO THE MOUNTAINS

Mangart

N ext morning we walked down to scratch the pigs and then packed the bike ready for our trip over to the Triglev national park. I had found another apartment in another small village called Ratece and hoped it would be as nice as the one slowly vanishing from view in our wing mirror. This was another short trip of only about 80 miles but as is our want we stopped for coffee, stopped to wander a village, stopped to stare at Griffon vultures, stopped for more coffee, stopped to chat with strangers, and stopped just because we wanted too. We eventually ended up on the main drag to Kranjska Gora and saw more cars, motorbikes, and people than we had seen on the whole trip so far. Our village was within walking distance of the Italian border and turning onto the small off ramp I knew it was going to be fine because we were held up by an old red tractor and an even older old woman driving it.

Our apartment faced a wild meadow and apple orchid with the mountains forming a long line beyond. In the morning they were a stunning white/ grey and in the evening a rose red. We had the use of a small garden overlooking all this and the air was filled with wild life. One morning a group of Griffon Vultures circled and climbed higher and higher over us on the thermals gaining enough height to soar over the mountains in the distance. We watched each day as an old couple and their shot-putter of a daughter cut sections of the meadow with a scythe for the huge shaggy brown cows back in the barn. Much as we love the bike it was so peaceful and beautiful we had to virtually force ourselves to get our bike gear on, the heat didn't help much either.

Looking at the map I noticed that just outside of the village a road led up to a place called "The three country border" where you could simply step into Italy, Slovenia, and Austria, and we decided we should have a ride up. As it was only a kick and a spit up the mountain I would have been content to go up in my shorts but our lass being the sensible one refused to even think of it. She is right of course, back in the day I would ride my 1200 Bandit in boots, shorts, and a tee shirt, but then I got rear ended (fortunately when I had all my gear on) and I can see the sense of her stance.

Bloody hell, I have no idea who named the pot holed crumbling knee deep gravel strewn dirt track we went up a "road" but he seriously needs some sort of slapping. There were signs of it being repaired, well I saw a rusty shovel stuck in the hedge, but nothing could be done about the drainage ditches that were dug horizontally across the road. Ah It was fun I have to admit, and coming back down was even funnier. The views up there were magnificent and the hills are covered in Lupins, bloody Lupins! This kept Theresa very happy and she insisted on showing me all the photos of them. Lovely.

Next day we decided to get up early to beat the heat because we were going too ride up to the Mangart Pass. This is an amazing and (look I know I use the word "amazing" a lot while describing places in Slovenia but if you go you will understand and forgive me) staggeringly beautiful region. The ride up there is one of the great rides in Europe but it just gets better when you finally reach the top. You have to pay to ride this road but it's only about €2 and even I would pay double (see how good it must be?).

An amazing ride up to amazing views.

What I didn't expect was that we would have to park lower than the summit because the road was blocked due to sodding snow. Oh how our lass laughed. So we stripped off, put our shorts on, (road blocked by snow and yet we were still sweating cobs just getting our bike gear off, that's just not right) and trudged up the bloody mountain, I made our lass carry the sandwiches. Because of the road being blocked we had virtually the whole mountain range to ourselves. Sitting there eating lunch in shorts and a tee shirt while throwing snow balls at each other and looking over the Julian Alps will be a memory that will stay with me forever. For that memory alone I thank the whole cosmos for giving me that strange twisted desire to ride a bloody motorbike.

As if all that wasn't enough we also have The Vršič Pass, or highway 206, or The Russian road. No matter what name you want to call it the word's that will pass your lip's once you have rode round it will be ... yeah you guessed it, "That was bloody amazing". Look, you have to go, seriously. Sitting here writing about it my guts are tight and my face is split in a huge idiotic grin just remembering the time we have spent there. One thing though, if you do go don't tell everyone about the place or it will end up like those overhyped and overcrowded roads in Italy.

I overcooked this corner and she got a very blurred picture down the side of the mountain.

The next two days were so hot we decided to give

the bike a rest and have a wander around the area. We followed the turquoise river and explored the wooded hills where we discovered a small lake bubbling with underground streams. We walked up to a huge ski centre along an old railway line and tried to keep track of how many different types of birds and butterflies we saw. We walked amazing paths, ate amazing food, and drank amazingly cold beer, and what's more every moment was amazing. That's the last time I am going to use the word "Amazing" in this book.

In life sometimes it's not who you are or where you are it's just being there at the right moment. We paused on one of our walks and just happened to be in the exact place at the exact moment an Eagle lurched out of a tree not twenty feet from us. It glared at us as it dragged its huge body into the air. A perfect moment, you seem to get a lot of those when you travel on a motorbike.

Where we stayed; Apartma Andrej. 29a Rateče, 4283 Rateče, Slovenia.

Verdict; this was a big apartment and we even had a washing machine and posh coffee maker with free coffee. They let us in early and even provided us with tea and cake (because we are English presumably) while the husband finished off cleaning the place. The bedroom looked out over the meadow and mountains so our lass made me bring her tea in bed every morning so I could open the curtains onto that view and she could just lay there in silence drinking her tea, drinking in that perfect view. The rooms were large, the bed also, and the bike was parked on the drive way. The place was good, but the view was magnificent and the best reason to stay there.

Our place was down there and on the left.
What a view to wake up to.

LORD OF THE FLIES

The Gross-thingy Pass.

We took our time packing the next morning partly because we had another easy day and partly because we couldn't tear ourselves away from the place. We were heading for the Gloskno ...Glongrockner ... oh bloody hell the Grossglockner pass but as it was Sunday and we figured it might be a bit crowded I decided to split the journey there so we could ride over it early on the Monday morning. The ride was brilliant, snow-capped mountains, waterfalls, great coffee, twisting roads, and friendly bikers. I found a reasonably priced room in the village just before you pay the toll for the pass and it turned out to be another winner. Our bedroom window looked right out and down into a river valley with the mountains forming a wall at the end. We even had a balcony. Just down the hill was an amaz ... wonderful restaurant where we sat outside and ate under an umbrella because it suddenly started belting down with rain. I must at this point admit I was getting converted from kebabs and anything cheap to actually paying money for decent food.

The view from Haus Marienheims terrace.

Where we stayed; Haus Marienheim. Hof 73, 9844 Heiligenblut, Austria.

Verdict; A handy place to stop just before you pay the toll for the Grossglockner so you can have a full day wandering over the roads, view was great and although it was one of the more expensive places (€46 for a double) I didn't leave feeling I had been gypped.

I suppose some people would say it's just a road.

The Grossglockner, well what can I say, nothing that hasn't already been said I suppose so I will hand you back over to Theresa.

Monday, up early, early breakfast of cheese and ham. Off to ride the Grossglockner. It is very difficult to describe how staggering the road was. It was the most beautiful road I have ever been on. Hair pin bends, waterfalls, snow, sheep, goats, and I even saw a Marmot!! Glad we got up early as it was cooler up there and there wasn't much traffic. Loads of viewing places, took hundreds of photos.

(Theresa hardly ever holds on and is constantly taking videos and pictures when we are in the mountains, she's quite a dab hand at it now, but she still squeals when we really hammer the corners).

Rode on through the Krimmler pass and stopped at the Krimmler waterfall. We stopped again a few miles further on and could still hear it. Apparently because of the amount of snow still on the mountain there is far more water coming down than normal, even the locals are driving to see it.

Okay I can't just leave it to our lass because that road really is one of the most magnificent rides I have ever been on. There is no way you can just ride through it, you have to keep stopping just to try and drink it in. My one regret is I don't live closer to it so I could just ride it, just ride over it and concentrate on how the tyres stick to the road, the perfect corners, the flowing cambers, and the sheer exhilaration you feel just being there. I love being a bloody biker.

We stopped for the night in Strumm and I would advise you to bypass it if you are in the area at that time of the year. Our farm stay was great, the owner was lovely, the breakfast was huge, and the town was pretty but my God the flies. Seriously it was on biblical bloody proportions, I fully expected Moses to appear and demand we let his people go. Flies in the restaurant, in the café, in the shop, in the bedroom, in the dining room, in the toilet, thousands of the buggers. When we got back to our room our lass made me go on a murder rampage before we went to bed and the slaughter was carried out with precision and cold determination. I can still see her eyes glinting as the thunder crashed around us and hear her whispers in my head "Kill them, kill them Chris, kill them all". The really weird thing is nobody else took any notice of them, they just pretended the damn things weren't there, It got quite spooky in the end.

Oh and we got charged €10 for two bloody awful coffees. Don't ask me how this happened as the memory is still far too painful to talk about. Fortunately Theresa was paying, but it still hurt.

Where we stayed; Maurachbauer. Obisdorfweg 7, 6275 Stumm, Austria.

Verdict; A classic farm stay and without those damn flies it would have been lovely, in fact it was lovely even with the bloody things. There's a barn to park the bike in and the house itself is beautiful. The woman who runs it is well worth making friends with as she is a very interesting person in her own right. Breakfast was a huge affair with a lot of homemade produce.

Strumm, they are there, you just can't see them.

The next day was a trip through some beautiful countryside and at any other time it would have ticked all the boxes for a nice ride, unfortunately it was a little like meeting a gorgeous looking woman and taking her for a meal only to discover she wants to go to a vegan restaurant. All the elements were there but because of where we had come from it just seemed a little, well disappointing I suppose. It was okay to start with but the further we went from the mountains the more normal it became. Eventually I pulled over into a layby with a good view behind of the mountains we were leaving and parked the bike.

Birds were singing, the sun was shining and we wandered back along the road for Theresa to get a good picture of the route we were leaving. I rolled a cigarette and cast a jaundiced eye around our surroundings. "That will be a nice picture" I said to her looking off into the distance. "Yeah, now I want one of the bike, I'm just waiting until that old tractor working in the field gets alongside it" she said staring over my shoulder. I turned slowly and placed my arm around her. I had parked the bike tight up against the field in question because I had thought the same thing and intended to take a picture of our steed as well.

Having spent some time growing up on a farm I recognised the tractor for a very old Massey Ferguson, my grip tightened around Theresa's waist as I also recognised what it was pulling. "Chris, you're hurting" she said pulling a little away. "It's a feckin muck spreader" says I setting off on a skip run walk towards the bike and trying to tell myself it would be foolish to expend undue energy when my fears were groundless. The tractor was now a few hundred yards behind the bike, it slowed, and I heard it engage the PTO. I now gave up the skip run walk method of travel and belted towards my precious Susie fingers desperately scrabbling in my pocket for the keys. The tractor was drawing ever closer on its relentless course and suddenly the theme tune from "Mission im-bloody-possible" started up in my head. I leaped onto the bike, thrust the keys into the ignition and quickly turned to see it the tractor driver was only having a bit of a joke all in one fluid movement. He wasn't even looking at me, the shit was flying in a graceful ark closer, ever closer and I smiled over at our lass as I turned the key. The feckin thing stuck. I turned it back, and tried again, it stuck again.

Our lass started running towards either me or the tractor and then I saw her pace slow, she backed off, I was on my own (I also vowed in that instant never to offer her the last place in a lifeboat). I could now smell not only the liquid slurry, but my own fear. The clattering of the spreader's teeth were thundering in my ears, sweat was running down my neck, I took the key out, spat on it, thrust it back in and turned. The timer must have reached two seconds as the bike fired up and I rammed it into gear. Theresa had her hands on her knees doubled over with laughter. I leapt off the bike, my eyes alight with excitement, "I was Tom Cruise" I said standing proudly before her. "Yes, yes you were honey" she said patting my shoulder. The tractor driver never stopped and due to the smell now lingering in the air we departed rather swiftly also.

When we halted for lunch I asked her if she had taken any pictures of the incident. The reply was in the negative because apparently the look on my face was so amusing she had forgotten all about her camera. This was the second time she had failed to record a moment in my life due to her finding my predicament so amusing. The first was in Barcelona when a street entertainer made me stand on his shoulders and then paraded up and down the Ramblas with me still up there.

OH YEAH …
GERMANY

We stayed the first night in Germany on a horse farm which should have had flies but didn't. I had a nice pizza, our lass had a crap lasagne and when we got back she made friends with one horse and an enemy of another, oh and we had a row.

As I mentioned earlier in the book our lass is great and 99.9% of the time we just sail along on a sea of contentment and happiness. But (and there is always a but in life) because it's so good, when things go wrong it really is bloody awful. We never argue about the big things, she never moans when I come home from the bookies drunk and skint (I don't gamble or even drink anymore) and I don't wave clothes bills at her and demand to know where all the money has gone (she is as frugal as me and it's her money anyway so why would I care). No, we argue over something so pathetic that it would be funny if it was in a sitcom. We once fell out for two days over the size of a volume button on her mobile phone, I kid you not. Now an argument isn't so bad if it's over a big thing ("I promise to never wear your dress again Theresa" or "Chris it wasn't the whole rugby team, the prop forward was busy") because those things can be worked out. When it's something tiny it's hard to actually discover the real reason for the fall out and fix it.

Having an argument at home is bad enough but when you are away on a motorbike for five weeks it's not only worse because you are on holiday and supposed to be having a great time, but it can be downright dangerous. You can't ride angry, you just can't. You can't ride simmering about something that the person sat behind you has done or said because all your judgement, skill, and road craft vanishes. Sort it out before you get on that bike, seriously, it might just save your life.

Arguments (especially ours) arise out of nowhere and I think that's a basic flaw in human evolution, surely we should have developed some warning sign like the theme to "Jaws". You could come down to breakfast and just vaguely hear it in the back of your mind, you say "Good morning darling" and it gets slightly louder. This would give you time to back off and rack your brains for whatever it is she thinks you have done.

All this was supposed to lead up to tell you about why we had that argument in the middle of nowhere and how we managed to put it right but I can't for the life of me remember what the hell it was about or even how we did put it right. All I can remember is getting a text from her saying "I can see a deer's bottom" and everything was alright again. So, no life lesson or advice for you there my mate I am afraid.

Anyway, I just wanted you to know touring with your partner can be hell on occasions so when it is get the bugger sorted ASAP, and definitely before you set off on the morning.

Where we stayed; Allgäu Meadow Ranch. Engelitz 2, 88145 Hergatz, Germany.

Verdict; an interesting place to lay your head and we enjoyed it. Good room, good breakfast, nice area, and it's full of horses and goats. What more could you want.

We were heading for Freiburg and decided to spend a couple of nights there because our lass likes trams and I had also found a rather interesting hostel to stay at which was cheap. Heading off we struck traffic, not just normal traffic but mile after mile of solid traffic, nothing was moving in either direction. I love filtering and it's very rare to have morons trying to block you when you are in Europe (unlike our own country) so we still managed to move along at a decent pace. Eventually (and I mean eventually) we found the cause of the problem. It seems there had been a crash in a tunnel and coming to the front of the queue we realised we were going nowhere. This is where a motorbike comes in handy because there was a small gap in the central barrier and after a moment's hesitation we just zipped through it onto the other side of the road, found a turn off, and continued on our way.

Lovely.

We didn't ride any autobahns after that and stuck instead to the small roads passing lakes and little villages. Now this was a nice ride and we enjoyed it but for some reason a small incident can stand out in your memory and remain with you. We were riding through a heavily wooded area and I pulled into a stopping place to enjoy the shade for a little while (it was still bloody baking).

It was just a normal stopping place with nothing of any real value but for some reason it was a magical moment. We were alone and traffic only passed sporadically leaving only the sounds of the forest to surround us. A large area where you turn off had been left to grow wild and it was covered in wild flowers and meadow grass, it was alive with the sound of crickets, the smell of the flowers, and the air was filled with butterflies. Theresa wandered off, in her element, I took my jacket off and sat down on the kerb.

Look I have lived a bit of a life my mate, I was what you might call lost to the dark side for a while in my youth and if there really are pearly gates I wouldn't put up an argument if they never let me through them. Having said that as I sat there listening to my bike slowly ticking in the half shade of those huge trees and watching my Theresa wandering gently through that meadow grass with her arms stretched out I bloody cried, I sat there with a fag in my gob and silent tears dripping from my eyes in total and abject happiness.

Abject because I couldn't reconcile why my life could be so wonderful after doing so many wrongs, and happy because maybe, just maybe, in life there really can be redemption.

*Blubbered my bloody eyes out here,
big Jessy that I am.*

When our lass came back she put her arms around me and asked me what was wrong. "Nowt, just being a twat" I said. "Lunch" she said taking me by the hand and leading me back towards the bike. "Too feckin right" I said kissing her and slipping back into my jacket.

We stopped at a restaurant tucked away in the Black Forest for lunch with views to die for and drifted through the afternoon in a daze of contentment.

Our hotel was on the outskirts of Freiburg right opposite the tram stop and it looked as strange in real life as it had in the photos. The "Gasthaus Waldheim" it was called and just like a book, you shouldn't judge it by its cover. The words eclectic and eccentric don't do it justice and again, if you are in the area it's a great place to stay even just for the breakfast. We had arrived a little early and there was no sign of life so we ditched the bike and wandered through the town gate to seek coffee. The area around the hotel is backed by steep wooded hills and the ride in had been beautiful so we were in a pretty chilled out mood, even the price of the namby pamby organic coffee failed to alter my mental demeanour. There is something to be said for just sitting, just kicking your legs out and sprawling for an unspecified amount of time while watching the world go by. There is also something to be said for getting value for money from a coffee so I nicked as much sugar as I could.

Eventually we walked back down to the hotel to be greeted by the elegant cigar smoking eighty year old lady owner. I have gone on about the hotel so won't go on about it again, in fact I have racked my brains as to how I could describe it and came up empty, just don't miss the chance to stay there if you wander past. There is also a fantastic restaurant just up the road where we ate both nights, the food and service were brilliant, the "Kybfelsen" I think you call it.

Sometimes it's good to just pause so the next day we set off on the tram to explore the town and on our arrival were greeted by a huge group of primary school children presenting a play in the square, we couldn't tear ourselves away because it was so funny. We wandered the city then walked slowly back to the hotel along the river and into the hills behind, stopping for a coffee that cost a fortune at some sort of cooperative allotment society (and there wasn't even any sugar to nick).

I have always looked upon crossing Germany as something of a chore to be done as quickly as possible; I really need to get out of this mind set. The people are friendly, the roads are good, and the places I have stayed have been great but nothing has ever happened to make it stand out as a destination in itself. I suppose we all have our favourites.

Where we stayed; Pension Waldheim. Schauinsland-strasse 20, 79100 Freiburg im Breisgau, Germany.

Verdict; I think I have said it all in the above description and will leave it at that apart to say again how much we liked staying there, and it was cheap as well.

ZONE BLANCHE

Hotel-Restaurant du Windstein

We don't have a television at home but I do pay for "Amazon prime" so we watch films and TV series on that (we hate the amount of adverts on TV and have no interest in sport so it ticks all the boxes for us) and one night I came across a series from France. It's called "Black Spot" on Amazon for some reason despite it being called "Zone Blanche" in France. I bet they wouldn't rename "Pulp Fiction" into "Respectable novels to read that will inform and educate the reader". Anyway I digress, so we started watching and it's a little dark but also quite funny in parts, which is what we like, the thing that really got to our lass though was the setting. It's set in a village called "Villefranche" amidst huge gloomy dank forests that stretch for mile after mile and small twisting wet roads (it rains in every episode) link isolated rundown villages that are populated by, well if you have ever spent time in "The Forest of Dean" you will get an idea of the characters in the series.

One night after a particularly gruesome murder by something that lives in the forest our lass pipes up "I don't know where they filmed this but I wouldn't want to spend a night there". Now she said the same thing about crossing the Australian outback after watching "Wolf Creek" and on that one I have to admit I agreed with her.

I made a mental note to find out where the series was filmed, it looked a bit like the Vorges area but I needed to make sure. I patted myself on the back, it was indeed the Vorges and I immediately started looking to see how I could work it into the trip.

Lying in bed the night before we were due to set off into France I snuggled up to our lass and in the dark of the night I stroked her hair and whispered into her ear "Guess where we are going tomorrow my lovely" She shifted and relaxed into me sighing dreamily, "Somewhere nice I bet". "We go to ...

"Villefranche". She twisted round in a flash and gave me a slap on the head. "You bloody bugger" she said pretending to laugh, but I could see the terror in her eyes and smell the fear.

Now I had travelled all over France but for some reason never had call to visit the area we were heading for. I had toured the "Ballons des Vorges" but never set my tyres down in the north Vorges right in the top eastern corner of France, always either heading north before I got there or turning due south to pass Verdun and loop round, this was a big mistake on my part as it turned out.

I had found what looked like the perfect place to stay for a few days, "The hotel Restaurant du Windstein". Now it did admittedly look a little run down, and it did admittedly look like it was stuck out in the middle of nowhere, it was also suspiciously cheap, in fact it was everything I was looking for to give Theresa a real taste of "Zone Blanche" … (Chris paces the room and sniggers as he rubs his hairy talon like hands together).

Excerpt from Theresa's diary.

"Long journey across the border into France but all the names are still in German, very confusing. Eventually get to our hotel. It's on its own in the forest. There is one neighbour across the road but their house looks weird. The hotel looks weird as well. We knocked but no one came so I suggested we walk round the back and we found a note "Chris room 7" and a key, so we went in. The owner was sat at the bar with a friend drinking

and simply waved his hand pointing upstairs. Very dark hallway even in the daytime, our room is okay. A lot of the plants are dead in the garden. There is a cat with three legs, and it only has one eye".

My mate, the three legged one eyed cat.

What Theresa fails to mention was her reaction to our shared bathroom facilities. After she had found it she told me I should go have a look. I was in stitches, it was a broom closet with a quarter bath and a shower head. On the subject of accommodation our lass is a brick, as long as it's clean she will put up with anything (never stay at the "Delebab" in Budapest, it's the only hotel our lass has immediately walked out of) and fortunately this place was (although not a palace) immaculate so I knew I was at least holding my own.

Having rid ourselves of our bike gear we went downstairs to see if lunch was being served and to have a drink.

The owner spoke very little English but was friendly and the menu was only in French or German but we got the gist and plonked ourselves down to wait. Oh bloody hell it was gorgeous, seriously gorgeous, and Theresa broke into a smile. After lunch we went outside to survey our surroundings. A small twisting road in, a small twisting road out, and trees, thousands of trees, more trees you could shake a stick at, and there were plenty of sticks being as there were so many trees. There was a small path across the road with a sign pointing to the "Ruine du Nouveau Windstein" and we set off to explore it not expecting much. It was like walking into a fairy tale, an old castle, thick dark woods, wildlife heard but not seen, and we had it all to ourselves. We did have a bit of a row because I acted like a knob but that just gives us a good excuse to go back one day to make it perfect.

Getting back I decided to give the bathroom a go and discovered if you squat in a quarter bath in a broom closet with a shower head in your hand you immediately start talking Japanese. For some reason I became a Samurai warrior and treated

Theresa to my new found language skills when I returned to the room. She called me an idiot and refused to pander to me. (I have since remembered watching one of Akira Kurosawaone's films and that's where I got it from, my God that makes me sound sophisticated!)

Excerpt from Theresa's diary.

Bloody hell what a day, brilliant breakfast, bread beautiful bread. Huge white loaf and seeded brown, homemade jams and local meats. Rode to "Fleckinstein" castle. An amazing place, we were first in and had it to ourselves. Two broods of Falcons live in the ruins and we watched them soaring and feeding their chicks. Views for miles over the forest. Then we visited the Maginot line, my God it was just fascinating, 3km underground and 12c. Tunnels, train lines, bunkrooms, kitchens, hospitals, air cleaning plants, power stations, just like a small town underground".

I can concur about the Maginot line, it really was fascinating and it really brings that period of terrible conflict to life. Now I had always been taught that its construction was a total waste and that the Germans just ignored it and waved as they simply drove around the fortifications, and yet talking to one of the guides there I gained a rather different view. The trouble with history is that we always tend to view it from our point of view. Our guide pointed out (from a French point of view) that the Maginot line was actually successful in the purpose for which it was built. This was the way he explained it;

After the terrible suffering the First World War brought to the country's involved France had to look at the defence of its borders and try to prevent anything like that from happening again. They had a few problems, the war had taken a huge toll on the population (1 in 20 had been killed) and this left gaps not only in society as a whole but a particularly acute shortage of men suitable for defence of the country. They were also skint, now building the Maginot line was expensive (3 billion Francs) but not as expensive as maintaining a huge and well equipped army to defend that area over an unspecified and indefinably prolonged time scale. The other reason was an issue of trust, France just wasn't sure if Germany invaded again that Britain would actually come to its defence and so needed to force the Germans up into Belgium so as to add another country into the mix. This last point sounds bloody awful, but it is understandable. So was it a total failure, I suppose just like most things, the truth is less important than your own viewpoint on it.

We spent a long time with the guide and he did a great job, even showing us the mechanical lifting system for the gun and observation turrets in action. I watched mesmerised as the huge beams lifted the machine gun turret up to ground level. The complexity, the engineering required and sheer scale of the construction had me enthralled. Then it dawned on me, all this effort, all this technology and innovation was put into place to simply enable one person to kill another person more efficiently, something we have been doing from the first time someone picked up a rock. No wonder I'm an anti-social git.

We shook hands with our guide and for a while discussed the state of the world (that was code for talking about "Brexit" by the way) before entering the sunlight again. Outside we had a chat to a couple of Polish bikers lovely couple and we had even visited their home town amazingly enough) and I placed the key into the bike and turned. It again refused to turn, no matter what I did it refused to budge a feckin millimetre. Now that could have been a bugger, miles from our hotel, even further away from home, and bugger me, no phone signal. That could have put the mockers on the whole holiday. It wasn't a problem of course because I always carry a spare key in my jacket pocket. I don't leave it at home or in the hotel room or tent, I always carry it with me. Take a spare key my mate and keep it with you.

Another place I didn't mind paying to get into.

I put the new key in and we set off back to the hotel feeling rather pleased with myself. Now whenever some people go on holiday and you ask them how it was they will always at some stage come out with "Oh and we had such a funny waiter for our table ... ". I am afraid I am now going to be one of those people. We got back and our lass decided she wasn't hungry enough for tea but fancied a bit of cake. I wasn't too interested in this fact because I was down to my last grubs of tobacco and needed to acquire more at the earliest convenience. As we approached the bar we were presented with the first sight of the hotels waiter/barman/kitchen assistant. He was rather rotund and soft of face wearing a "Minny Mouse" tee shirt and wearing too tight shorts. Our lass asked if cake was available (it was) and I asked if cigarettes were available (they weren't). He noticed the frown of concern that crossed my face and reached behind him, "Here I have some, you may take enough until you ride the 30k to the nearest Tabac, here, for you" he says smiling over at me and pushing a bunch of long slim cigarettes into my hand. We retire to the terrace (three plastic chairs and a wobbly table around the back of the hotel) to await our cake.

"That was nice of him wasn't it" our lass says. "Yeah, he seems a lovely boy, menthol cigarettes obviously though" I say rolling one between my fingers and deciding I would fire it up immediately.

I had flicked my lighter and took my first deep drag just as he appeared around the corner with the cake. Unfortunately not having a menthol cigarette for over thirty years my brain had forgotten the effect one of the bloody things can have on you. Placing the cake on the table our waiter leaned close to my ear and placed his hand on my shoulder "Menthol, my friend, not for children" he says wagging his other finger at me as I leaned on the wall for support.

The cake was magnificent, a huge portion of homemade cherry and ice cream, and what's more we had made a new friend. He informed us about another castle just by his village (in fact the whole area was littered with castles each more beautiful and more romantically desolate than the last) that we should visit. He was the only gay in the village, something he seemed to take seriously and if there was ever a competition to find the kindest, and funniest, he would get my vote, he was and is, one of the rare people I took an immediate liking too.

Excerpt from Theresa's diary.

Lovely breakfast again and out to Falkenstein castle. Lovely walk through the woods, saw tree creepers and black woodpeckers (and the holes they make). Lots of lizards and an Eagle sat in a tree. Strange bright yellow mushrooms. The castle is built on sandstone rock with rooms and storage carved out. The erosion has left beautiful markings on the stone. Then on to Bitche Citadel, huge fortress, again built on rock with underground catacombs, billets, bakers, ammo storage, animal pens etc. We were supplied with headphones telling the story of the siege. It was colder and cloudy when we came out but still good views from the top. Another lovely day.

Now a word of warning if you ever visit that Falkenstein castle, in the place you park the bike you will see three clearly marked signs sending you off to various points. Take the one marked "Castle" and follow the plain and easy to follow trail through the woods and climb gradually until you reach another broader path. This broader path gets very steep and winds through dense forest for what must be at least a mile. As you turn a sharp corner you will come to a very long and very solid barbed wire fence where the path simply comes to a sodding end. Pause here to gather your breath, wipe the sweat from your brow, and resist the temptation to say "I knew this wasn't the way". Instead simply smile and retrace your steps a mile down that stony dusty tree root lined path to the post hidden in the undergrowth with the big sign attached saying "Castle this way".

We had a great stay in this area, and are already planning another trip back to explore more of it, I really recommend the hotel and the whole area, considering it's so close I am shocked at my stupidity for not finding it sooner.

Where we stayed; Hotel-Restaurant du Windstein. 8 Route Obersteinbach, 67110 Windstein, France.

Verdict; an amazing place to stay and don't be put off by the first sight of it. This I think ranks up there with some of the most memorable places we have laid our heads on any of our tours. Everything about the place was bordering on a weird state of excellence and I can't wait to go back.

LIFE AND DEATH

There is a place I find impossible to pass without stopping, a place I am un-ashamed to say that never ceases to have such an emotional impact on me I find it impossible to leave that place without tears filling my eyes. I wrote a book a while back and mentioned in it my reaction to the first ever sight of this poignant and moving place. This is what I wrote.

The next morning I woke very early and set off for the Ossuaire de Douaumont and the battlefield of Verdun. It should have been cold, damp, and foggy but it was a beautiful summer's morning and somehow that made it all the more devastating when I pulled around the corner and saw that huge monolithic monument rising up in front of me. I parked the bike and as I swung off I caught sight of the field of white crosses and I cried, Christ so many crosses. I walked in silence around the site and would suddenly burst into tears for no discernable reason, thank God there was on one else there to see me.

As we set off on the morning I had intended to follow the "route Sacre" from Bar le Duc up towards Verdun and then turn off for our hotel but I just couldn't do it with Theresa on the back. This wasn't because the route is some pot holed quagmire but simply because Theresa didn't know the significance or history of the route and I didn't want to give her some pathetic potted synopsis of its relevance to WW1. At least that's what I told myself, looking back I now understand the real reason, it was because I didn't want to put her through it as she tends to feel things as deeply as me, instead we rode past fields of corn and sunflowers in the sunshine.

Excerpt from Theresa's diary.

Another lovely breakfast. Paid for our stay and Chris said he would buy me some of their home made jam (banana orange and apricot). The owner gave us a jar for free. Bit of a long ride today but the scenery was lovely, fields of corn, wheat, rape, and sunflowers. The landscape was quite flat and the sky was beautiful. Stopped at a memorial for a village that was destroyed in WW1.

They had to abandon their homes because it was so damaged and polluted that they couldn't return. It was left as it was with craters and destroyed houses as a memorial. It was eerily quiet, not much bird song. They had rebuilt the church. Emotional. Saw plenty of eagles. Found our hotel, the river Muese runs right past it plus a canal. Three donkeys!

The village we were staying in was a slightly nondescript affair but the surroundings and the hotel made up for it. There was one café run for locals by a large happy French woman and her partner and a huge grain storage silo. No the grain silo didn't help run the café, what I meant was it was in the village. What made up for this lack of charm and amenities was that river and canal and on the evening we sat by the water and reflected on how lucky we were to have the life we were leading. Sometimes this fact overwhelms me and sitting there throwing small sticks into the slowly flowing river, watching the soft smile form on our lass's face as some bird or other called from a tree, and seeing the bike, my bike, my dirty rain and mud splattered lump of a bike that has brought me so much joy sitting in a dusty car park I felt feckin blessed, probably because I am blessed be buggered.

The next morning the sun shone and we made our way to Verdun and the purpose of our stay in the area.

As you turn off the main road at Charny sur Meuse and head into the wooded slopes it's impossible to not think of the devastation that once ebbed and flowed along these typical French towns. You climb higher along a road surrounded on both sides by woods until gradually through the branch's you catch glimpses of large mounds of earth, as if miners from long ago had dug for precious metals and left the forest to reclaim the damage they had done. Craters, shell holes, sometimes jagged rusted twisted girders, huge blocks of concrete serving no purpose litter the undergrowth. You turn a corner and there it is, towering over the trees like a huge concrete submarine, its massive white conning tower pointing upwards into the sunlight. To the left an immaculate hedge spreads in front of you along the road and you pull into the car park, getting off the bike you catch a glimpse, just a glimpse of some white crosses through a gap in the hedge.

You stand, pause, and stare at the Douaumont Ossuary, crossing the road the gap in the hedge widens as you approach and you see the few white crosses slowly multiple again and again, and again, and again, until all you can see are thousands of perfectly spaced crosses. 300,000 died here and the reality hits you as if someone has grabbed you by the back of your neck and forced you to see.

I had visited this place before but always by myself and I had tried to explain to Theresa how much it affected me without expecting her to feel the same range of emotions because that would make a sham of something pure and truthful, I needn't have been concerned.

I have visited the large cemeteries on the allied landing beaches and came away feeling sadness and wonder at the bravery and the loss, but here it is something greater, something even more emotional and for some time I was puzzled as to why this would be so. I think I understand now. I am unashamedly quoting from one of my previous books here because it's when I remembered this incident that I gained the insight.

I had stopped to admire a perfect view and I was just getting back on the bike when I saw a small ruined house with flowers planted in front of it. Curious, I walked across the road for a closer look and saw a plaque written in French, German, and English. During the advance of allied forces across France a group of twenty German solders surrendered to the local French partisans on that spot, the partisans stood them against the wall and shot them. The brutality of the event, the sight of the bullet holes, and the fact that I was stood in the very same place all those men were killed shook me, but what I took away from it, and what stayed with me, was the forgiveness on all sides witnessed by those freshly cut flowers. A little further down that mountain was an equally well kept memorial to a flight crew from Nova Scotia in Canada who crashed and lost their lives, I had visited Nova Scotia, I had friends there, and it affected me deeply to think those men from that place so far away had come all this way to die on a French mountainside.

Those two memorials hit me for six because they

placed the whole war, the sheer waste, the horror into something small enough to understand. When you say 300,000 died you can be amazed and shocked at the number but can't place that huge sum in the forefront of your mind. At Douaumont the crosses for the dead slowly multiply in front of your eyes, only gradually forming the whole sea of dead in front of you and allowing your mind to grasp the meaning, the true meaning of what was lost, humanity itself.

We paused as we left to spend some time at one of the destroyed and deserted villages scarred with the garbage of war but both of us felt we were intruders in some sad haunted tableau, so we left both wrapped up in our thoughts.

Distance and time tends to cure most things and when we stopped for dinner we were still aware of the suffering and horror of the past, but living in our present once again.

Excerpt from Theresa's diary.

Out for a walk along the river it's beautiful. Wheat fields stretching to the horizon in a waving golden haze. Trout in the river. Had our picnic, saw an otter, a king-fisher, a white throated dipper, and a tern. Walking back saw another otter nearer the bank, somehow made up for the emotional morning.

I had been keeping the next stay secret from Theresa because I was hoping it would be a little special. I really was hoping because I had paid over €50 a night to stay there and no amount of sugar stealing could make up that amount if it was crap.

Where we stayed; Chambres dhôtes Logette. 33 rue du port, 55110 Consenvoye, France.

Verdict; Yeah it was fine, owners were nice, room was good and the shower was massive. The only problem was we were measuring it by the last place and that took some beating. There was a small kitchen available if you needed it.

PUSHING THE BOAT OUT

It was bloody baking the next day, even at 9am as I humped the panniers over to the bike and dropped them over the seat it was baking and I cast an envious glance at a young lad whizzing past in shorts and flip flops on his scooter. "If he comes off he will be ripped to pieces" I heard our lass comment as she arrived with the helmets. I made a non-committal "Humph" sound and shucked my sweaty armour clad jacket onto the dry dusty gravel.

"There's no rush honey, I will be a couple of minutes yet" I said seeing her doing her jacket up. Now I don't know if it's me but "a couple of minutes" is in fact "a couple of minutes" and as I was stood there fully kitted up waiting for her to saunter back from the canal, pick up her jacket from the seat, place her helmet on, and enquire if I wanted to see the picture of the ducks she had just taken I pondered on the fluidity of time. Eventually she looked ready and I plonked myself on the seat feeling the heat from it rise into my buttocks and desperately wanted to have the illusion of a cool breeze on my face. Her glasses were in her pocket, she needed her bag in the top box, she dropped her glove, her trousers were sticking to her and she needed extra time to hoist her leg over the saddle, sweet Mary and Joseph will it never end.

"Ready darling?" I enquire. "Yes, all ready" she says with a sweet smile.

That last exchange would only happen in a work of fiction, this is the truth of the matter.

"For fecks sake Tee I am feckin baking here, where have you been?"

"You said you would be a while sorting the bike out so I went to see the river"

"I said two minutes for fecks sake"

"You were over twenty minutes and I know because I looked at my phone for the time, don't get funny with me just because you're hot, I'm hot as well you know"

"Fecks sake" this last aside murmured under my breath as I hit the starter.

Five minutes later just as we have left the village behind us I reach back and squeeze her leg, she gives me a hug, and all is well again.

We rode past fields of poppy's, wheat and corn, the sun beat down and the bike did what a bike does best, gave joy to its riders.

Lunch time came and in the distance we saw a café on the corner of a crossroads, just a café, no houses no farms, no other buildings, just fields of wheat as far as the eye could see. We pulled onto the small patch of ground that served as a car park and stopped. I had ended up in a dip with my front wheel facing the wall. This may seem something of no consequence but even though the house salad was a magnificent affair, even though the staff and customers were a really friendly funny bunch, and even though life was sweet, all I could think about was how I was going to get that sodding bike out of that dip without looking like a numpty. One of the customers left, excellent, I could now maybe ride it out, bollox another car takes its place. Theresa shows little signs of making a move. "Fancy another coffee honey?" I say. I give up in the end when the owner of the other car orders food and settles in for the day. So instead of leaving like a world weary adventure seeking motorbike rider with a cheery wave, I depart like a clown pulling tugging and sweating over a useless lump of stubborn metal. Eventually and to some good natured sarcastic clapping we arrange ourselves on the seat. We did indeed give a cheery wave, I still felt like a twat though. To adjust my mind set I stopped at a small memorial a little way up the road and our lass read the inscription. The reason there was a crossroads in the middle of nowhere was simple, it used to be the main road into a village, the village now only existed in some old person's memory, destroyed and levelled in WW2 for some infraction the populace had committed.

Further up the road we turned off to visit a German war cemetery, black crosses, 30,000 dead fighting for something only the select few believed in, the rest either caught up in the lie or simply fighting because they felt they had to. I never know whether to feel more angry than sad.

A roundabout in the middle of nowhere, two tanks and a huge memorial to a battle that took place on that spot, more ghosts.

Pulling a bike out of a dip, Christ in the scheme of things, that's a pretty pathetic thing to get wound up about.

Theresa was indeed suitably impressed with my choice of hotel, I was bloody astounded. You ride up to it along a tree lined drive and the hotel overlooks the Chateau de Blerancourt, which houses the newly renovated Franco-American Museum (we never went in because we both yawned when read-ing the description of what was inside). Bloody hell what a bath, it was bigger than our front room at home (okay maybe not, but you get the idea) and the bedroom was a pleasure to sleep in. The food was once again just amazing, seriously, and I never begrudged paying the €26 for the three courses for a moment. We dined on the terrace and drank beer looking out onto the Chateau as the sun went down feeling very content with our lot. The village itself gives you a nice walk with plenty of old farm and town buildings to wallow in, there is also a huge old orphanage, we both decided not to look up its history as the last couple of days had just about drained every last scrap of empathy out of us and we couldn't face more sorrow and pain.

As I was checking the village on "Google" I just happened to come across a one star review for the local Tabac, *"Home deplorable, on the phone for these personal meetings. Change your profession! A shame!!"* Intrigued I checked the rest of the reviews (I have left the translation alone as I think it adds a little charm to the emotions expressed).

"Friendliness leaves at home a pity in a small village".

"Bar tobacco not friendly especially commercial not amiable with their customers before this bar ran well, it's a pity".

"The boss extremely unpleasant! No hello, no goodbye. Annoyed to give me change. On the phone all the time !!! I hallucinated the behaviour of this gentleman!"

"*Convenient to buy cigarettes, but do not look for friendliness or friendliness. What to say about opening hours.*"

"*He only just deserves to exist not merchant not kind not professional*".

"*As I regret the old managers! The boss is rude to the impossible; I have never seen such rudeness. No wonder his bar is always empty! A piece of advice, change your profession, trade is incompatible with your behaviour*".

"*The manager is not at all friendly, very difficult to say hello and goodbye to his customers! I do not recommend it at all! Change your job!!!*"

I immediately made it my task to visit this establishment and dragged Theresa away from a lavender bush she was enraptured with (it had hundreds of bees on it apparently). Theresa could sense my excitement and made me pause before we entered the café, I was virtually hopping from foot to foot.

Sometimes life can be cruel, sometimes all your hopes are dashed and you have to pick yourself up again. Here's the review I left.

"*Asked for coffee, I got coffee. Asked for tobacco, I got tobacco. Okay the owner isn't full of the joys of spring but the coffee was good and he even said goodbye*".

Theresa took my hand as I walked dejectedly back to the hotel, "But I thought it was going to be really horrible" I said with a sigh feeling confused. "I know honey, but sometimes life can't always go the way you want" she said trying to hurry me back to the bees.

We spent the next day just chilling as it would be our last day in France and we had to be up and gone early the next morning to catch the ferry, I checked the bike over, oiled the chain, added a bit of the stuff to the engine, and checked the tyres. If you are ever in the area this place is a good stop if you don't mind paying over €50 a night. I didn't regret it for a moment so that must say something.

Living the dream.

Where we stayed: Hostellerie Le Griffon. 22 Place du Général Leclerc, 02300 Blérancourt, France.

Verdict: This I think really was a great place to spend our last night in France. The food was magnificent and the hotel itself exuded charm so having such good staff

Chris Hardy

as well was a great bonus. The bike goes in a yard attached to the hotel that gets locked from 22.00 to 06.00.

ENGLAND'S
BOTTOM

I had booked a couple of YHA hostels for the return journey to Bristol, not that we needed to but simply to extend the break and see a couple of places we had never visited. One was on the South Downs and the other was another surprise for the lass.

I can remember turning to Theresa as we left the ferry, I can remember my exact words, and they still send a chill of horror down my spine. "I thought we could ride along the coast to the hostel honey, it might give us a nice ride for our first day back in good old England". I even smiled as I said it.

Oh for fecks sake, have you ever ridden along the coast rode from Newhaven to Shoreham on sea at 16.00 on a Friday evening in July? Have you? If you have why didn't you tell me? From the moment our tyres hit the tarmac we were transported into some hellish version of existence from a parallel universe. Who the feck are these people? Where do they come from? Roads rammed with over-priced overblown cars and their equally overblown owners all angry with life, pedestrians dressed in beach clothes their worst enemy had persuaded them they would look good in, look I have nothing against fat lass's but please for God's sake keep at least some clothes on, or at least don't wear those leggings that become transparent when they are stretched too far. My mates, I have had a bit of a hard life, I have lived in poverty and suffered shite you could not imagine so this is no middle class middle England rant but what the feck is going on in this country? In over five weeks I had not seen one drunk, on this road alone I must have seen over twenty staggering about, and I'm not talking about stag parties here. Litter spread over the pavements, vomit over the litter bins, cheap tat shops selling crap food and even crappier souvenirs. Is this our culture that we all hold so dear? For fecks sake I wanted to turn straight round and bugger off again, but I held my course, tried to block it all out, and told myself it was just reverse culture shock. It saddened me, it really did, and I apologise if you have taken offence but come on, anyway rant over, deep breath, find a happy place in your mind Chris.

The YHA was right up on the South Downs and provided a massive relief from what was happening below on the coast. It was peaceful, clean, and set in amazing countryside. I like staying at the YHA and have even wrote a book about how good they are for touring in this country, this one was no exception to the rule. We booked in, showered, ate, wandered the hills, and slept the sleep of the contented.

Where we stayed: YHA Truleigh Hill. Shoreham-by-Sea, West Sussex, BN43 5FB.

Verdict: As good as the ones I mention in my book "What … A Motorbike at a YHA?" … have I mentioned I wrote a book about touring on a motorbike and using the YHA as … okay I will shut up.

Next stop was a YHA near Stonehenge (we never called in, it's a pile of stones stood on end with a lot of funny looking people wandering around waving crystals and talking shite) and I was hoping our lass would get a kick out of it.

The hostel is attached to a rare breed's farm and it's free entry for hostel guests. Theresa loved it and

I have to admit I liked it too due to me spending part of my youth on a farm. They have rabbits and chickens and goats and cows and pigs and sheep and I am rambling now because the book is coming to an end and once it's finished I have to paint the sodding house.

Where we stayed: YHA Cholderton. Cholderton, Wiltshire, SP4 0EW.

Verdict: Lovely, decent parking for the bike, a nice big room, and loads of farm animals, look out for the flock of peacocks that sit on the roof.

HOME

The last leg was all of 50 miles, and it bloody rained. That's the thing about going away, as soon as the key turns in the door, as soon as you have put normal clothes on and spent a night in your own bed it's as if it never happened. Well that's what it's like for me but maybe that's because I am a Billy no mates, our lass wanders off and has coffee with her friends, I sit and look at a map or watch crap on "Netflix", roaming our two up and two down like Hamlet searching for the ghost of his father, and you know what? I wouldn't have it any other way.

Two things in my life saved me from taking a path that would have led down a very dark road, "Going Underground" by The Jam (a long story) and a motorbike. I can't think of anything else that has given me so much joy, so much excitement, and so many perfect moments in my life. Sometimes I will finish cleaning and servicing it and just stand staring at it. I pretend to be wiping oil from my hands, or rolling a fag, or fiddling with something that needs no fiddling with just so I can spend more time in its vicinity. When I tour solo I talk to the bloody thing, really talk to it, I have deep philosophical debates with it for God's sake.

I was once stuck in a bus stop miles from anywhere during a torrential rain storm in Andalucía with only a forlorn donkey for company. I was drenched, and forget "Sunny Spain", I was bloody freezing, I was also cold, tired, and on the verge of a depression. I sat slumped over smoking a damp badly made rolled cigarette wondering why the hell I was there. The thought of pitching a wet tent and spending another wet night in it filled me with something that could not be described as "Joy". At this thought I glanced over at the bag it was packed in on the back seat of the bike, and I immediately forgot about the tent. Seeing that wet tired looking grey lump leaning on its side stand with the rain pounding off it my face slowly began to form into a smile. My shoulders straightened and I kicked a sodden boot up onto the wooden bench while leaning an elbow on the knee of my drenched trousers, my smile widened. I began to snigger, then a full bellied gut aching thigh slapping unable to catch your breath laugh rose and filled that bus stop and even made the forlorn donkey raise its head. "You bastard, you drag me half way across Europe just to end up in a bus stop in a torrential bloody downpour, I hope you are feckin satisfied, I really sodding do" I managed to spit out between gasps for breath. The bike just sat there, and I knew I would rather be there with that ignorant lump of steel and plastic than anywhere else, or with anyone else in the world.

I don't know what it is, all the crap that gets spoken about "Freedom" and "being a rebel" or "living life on the edge" is just that, crap. Maybe it was true when they returned from WW2 or Vietnam in America but come on, let's not pretend. There is something though, something that drives us to get on the bloody thing in the first place against 99.9% of the populations advice. Then to drag your arse across a few thousand miles of unfamiliar roads in countries that drive on the wrong side of the road in search of places where English isn't spoken is a bit odd. To do it exposed to all that the elements can throw at you, either freezing, baking, or being thrust into the path of a bloody big articulated lorry by gale force winds is verging on the idiotic. So what is it my mate? What makes the thought of not having a bike so soul destroying, I think the only answer I can come up with is, it's just the way it is, so just sit back and accept it.

Oh by the way, continuing with the point about acceptance, a few days after returning I got a nice letter from the French police informing me I owed them £40 for speeding. I don't begrudge them this sum, it was a fair cop as they say, and I bear no ill will towards the Gendarmes or the French nation as a whole. However, ... *(I have deleted the following rant without Chris's knowledge as it covered almost three pages and was simply the sad ranting's of a man who hates to part with his money. Kind Regards, Theresa).*

The Triglav Mountains from afar.

TO SUM UP

Touring on a motorbike is special, from the moment you decide to go somewhere on it, even if it's only for a weekend, you experience a mind shift. An element of excitement enters into your life unlike anything else in your normal day to day existence. For me I can't even look at the thing without thinking it should be somewhere else other than sitting outside the house, it just doesn't seem to belong there, it looks out of place. Touring solo gives me something, I am sitting here trying to find the words to explain what it is and failing miserably, I am failing because when I am touring by myself there are moments that are so profound, they are almost religious in their intensity. Uplifting is the wrong word because that implies a lightening of the spirit, grounded is too staid, I think the only thing that comes close is a bit "new age" and I apologise for what's to follow, just be aware I have never worn sandals or a feckin kaftan in my life okay?

You become at one with yourself, with the world, your past, and your future.

You pause for a wee or a cigarette, pull over on a

small road miles from anywhere for a break and the silence surrounds you, for a moment your senses have to adjust,   and as you walk back to the bike it hits you. There is nothing else in the world other than you, the road, and that bike. You pause in mid step, nothing … else. You look at your hands, really look at them and see the things they have made, touched, and stroked, then you look at that feckin bike, and you see what it has shown you, where it has taken you, how much it has given you. You look around feeling slightly confused, an idiotic smile slowly starts to form on your face and you hear yourself whispering "Oh feckin yes". A moment later you yell the same thing with your arms outstretched. "OH FECKIN YES!" And that's when you realise nothing actually matters at all, you are in that moment, on that road, with that bike, and that's all that really, truly, exists.

I will now pause for a moment to light a sodding joss stick.

When I am touring with our lass the moments are totally different, we will be plodding along a road, nothing spectacular to look at and nothing of any interest happening when I get the urge to reach back and just squeeze her leg. In that moment a wave of happiness wash's over me, contentment, I suppose love would be the word to sum it up, not only love for the person, but love of what we are sharing together. There is something just as special about touring with a partner who loves being on the back, it's just a different kind of special. I love touring with our lass because we both fit, we complement each other, and if you have the same sort of relationship with whomever wants to go with you it's a blessing you should thank the gods for. If you haven't, for fecks sake don't let them within ten feet of that back seat.

So if you hear the words "Why don't I come with you?" take them along, you might just have as much fun as we do my mate.

...unless of course the road is blocked and they force you to hike up a bleeding great mountain that is, I can't see the fun in that.

STUFF I TAKE

As mentioned (or at least I think I did) here is a list of stuff I find useful to take along on any trip. If you have read any of my other books you might as well just skip this bit as it's always the same, apart that is from impressing the need to always take a spare key with you if possible and always keep it with you in a special pocket (it's no good back at the tent or in the hotel). This saved us on this trip and I am so glad I thought of it.

This list is the same no matter how long I go away for as it's nearly as big a pain in the arse breaking down in Bolton as it in in Barcelona. Try and keep it down as much as possible as it's all about attempting to cover as many eventualities without resorting to towing a bloody trailer.

Bike specific tool kit.

Go over the bike and make sure you have every Allen key, spanner, driver, and tool required to manage most tasks that could arise. Then check to make sure you have what's needed again. You are not going to be doing an engine rebuild on the side of the road so don't go mad, just try and take all the stuff that would or could get you out of trouble including anything odd you come across, I carry two springs from a Biro which are for ... you will remember if you have read my other book ...well they are for my starter switch because old V-Strom's have a stupid fault that you will come across eventually if you own one, so always keep a couple of these with you.

What I am saying is sometimes something will happen. You can't plan for all eventualities because life isn't like that. What you can do is just do the best you can, and if it's not enough, at least you know you did your best and you can then find a rock to sit on quite happily while you wait for the tow truck.

Hose repair tape. A small roll of this stuff could save the day.

Electrical tape. For obvious purposes.

Puncture repair outfit. For me it's the Stop and Go version. I also carry a few of the string type ones as you can jam more than one of these in to fix (God forbid) a bigger hole, and some CO_2 mini canisters. If you have an old tyre practice on it, watch a couple of YouTube's on how to do it and before you set off take it out and work through how you would do it, preferably wait for it to be raining and blowing a gale in a nice -4c.

Tyre pressure gauge. For stirring coffee, I jest of course.

Duct tape. I wrap a big wedge of the stuff around

my water bottles as it saves space and stops them clanking around.

A mini jump starter power pack. These things actually work. I have a DB power one and it's started the bike and can even start our lass's car. I really carry it so I can be a hero one day to a car load of Russian models. Strangely enough it doesn't seem to be that good at charging phones and the like but for its main purpose it's great.

A couple of phone power banks. These are great if you use your phone a lot for that Facebook thing. They can also run your sat nav when it's raining (unless you have one of those posh waterproof bike ones). Just always keep one charging on the bike.

Zip ties. I always end up using these things but can never remember what on.

Pouch containing spare bulbs, super glue, plastic cement, spare fuses.

12v Electric tyre inflater. I bought one from Aldi and then stripped the plastic surround off. I ended up with a tiny thing that packs away under the seat and chugs away quite happily when I use it. You can pay a fortune for a branded one that's twice the size if you so wish, or you can send me the money you saved by doing this. Don't leave it on the floor when in use though as it will bite your ankles, hang it up and let it swing.

Spare smart phone. Just an old one that has a very long battery life.

Spare oil. This does for the engine and the chain.

Stanley knife blades. Just to prove my Mam wrong about me playing with sharp things.

Strong elastic bands. Well why not and they do come in handy, I use them to keep the cable strapped in tight on my sat nav. I pick the ones up our postie throws on the floor, they are free, and I am doing my bit for the environment.

Now this sounds like a lot but if you ride a great bike like mine 99% of it will fit under the seat, including the electric pump.

Camping

Let's face it if you are on a bike you can only carry so much stuff. This stuff should be stuff that provides the maximum amount of use and comfort for the least amount of bother and bulk and the following list of gear fits in with these requirements for me. Again, this is the gear I use and it is perfect for me but you will have to find your own path because if you aren't comfortable when you are camping your life will be hell.

Vango Banshee two/three man tent. It packs down really well and has the bonus of having a door on either side for. Anything smaller and you will never fit all your gear inside, anything bigger and you are losing space, gaining weight, and creating work. Some take huge things with them. Fair plays, but all I want to do is sleep in mine, not hold a party or impress my neighbours.

1-2 season sleeping bags. I would like warmer ones but these pack down into the palm of your hand and if you leave your long-johns on you are warm enough (you did remember to pack your long-johns didn't you?) or if you have the space buy an old cheap one and take that as well, you can use it outside or as a shade attached to the bike.

Now at some stage it will rain and if you are lucky it will start once you are all set up and stop long before you have to leave. I am rarely lucky. This is where the Chamois leather you packed comes into play. Putting up a wet tent I use it to empty the water from the inside, packing up a wet tent I use it to clear the water off the outside. While in the tent listening to the rain read the book you brought or use that cheap Kindle you filled with free books off amazon. Listen to the albums you loaded onto your phone, Chill, the rain will stop ... eventually.

Klymit Static V sleeping mats. Expensive, but these also pack down to smaller than a bag of sugar, weigh bugger all, and are tough as old boots.

Cheap inflatable pillows. Yeah you can use your gear rolled up but a well inflated pillow is lovely. Don't put anywhere near as much air in as you think you need. Same goes for those sleeping mats.

OEX ultra lite camping chair. These are a bloody life saver. They fold down tiny but are strong enough and big enough to spend a long time just sitting in. Remember to take the cover off when you hit the sack as this stops anyone nicking them and they will also be dry for your morning coffee. Take a chair, really, you will be glad you did.

At some stage in the middle of the night, more than likely a cold wet one, you will want a wee. The toilet block is miles away and let's face it you just can't be bothered to traipse all that way, you are a bloke for Christ's sake, so what to do? Never urinate outside the tent, that's just nasty. Never try to wee into that coke tin, and never, never, try to wee into a narrow necked empty bottle of pop, the laws of physics are against you and you will instantly regret it but find there is no way to stop the disaster from happening in front of your eyes.

Always buy a bottle of apple juice (cloudy or clear it's your preference) before you camp for the night. These have a very wide neck suitable for the job in hand (see what I did there?). When finished you can leave said bottle outside the tent safe in the knowledge it will arouse no suspicion whatsoever unless you have been eating a huge quantity of beetroot. When leaving to perform your morning toilet you can carry the bottle with a swagger to dispose of the contents, after all who doesn't like a drink of apple juice while they shower?

Cooking gear is a two pot affair with foldable knives and forks. I also carry a chopped down frying pan when by myself. Cooking is done on a tiny folding Chinese stove that is a famous brand copy but even better than the original. I use a converter piece so I can use the cheap tall gas canisters.

Two 500ml water bottles fixed onto the bike (on the front crash bars) and two folding ones in the panniers. You can't have enough water and I drink a lot of coffee. I have never understood those camel back water things. The tubes must get filthy and why not stop for a drink?

Food. I take quite a bit of food with me when travelling alone because I am tight. I carry or buy along the way all the usual stuff as in bread, cheese, ham, fruit, etc. I also carry a few tins of sardines, some noodles, all-in-one porridge, three-in-one coffees from B&M (they are not the best but they are hot, sweet, and cheap as buggery) dried fruit, dried spicy sausage, and some **Trekmates dried adventure food packs** for emergencies. I love them, in fact I will eat them before I need them, I will find excuses to eat them, I will deliberately not buy food so I can eat them, avoid the Beef Hot Pot though, it's bloody awful.

When arriving on a camp site make friends with any group of German bikers. This group will not only be friendly but they will also invite you over to eat with them, provide you with ample free drink, laugh at all your jokes, and not bore you with how well they can ride. Do not worry about mentioning the war as they will mention it first. The polite response when they do bring it up is "Ah don't worry about it my mate, it could of happened to anyone".

And that's your lot, as they say.

Printed in Great Britain
by Amazon